A
DICTIONARY
OF
PHILOSOPHICAL
CONCEPTS

by
Dr. Russell A. Peterson

All rights reserved. No part of this publication may be reproduced, distributed, or transmitted in any form or by any means, including photocopying, recording, or other electronic or mechanical methods, without the prior written permission of the publisher, except in the case of brief quotations embodied in critical reviews and certain other noncommercial uses permitted by copyright law.

Printed in the United States of America

ISBN 978-1-941489-98-7

www.AudioEnlightenmentPress.com

TABLE of CONTENTS

DEDICATION	i
BOOKS and TRANSLATIONS by Dr. Russell A. Peterson	iii
PREFACE	v
DEFINITIONS	1 – 149
RESOURCES	151

IN
MEMORY
OF MY
FATHER

BOOKS and TRANSLATIONS

by
Dr. Russell A. Peterson

Translations

The God That Job Had

The Synoptic New Testament

The Modern Message of the Psalms

Children's Tales From Norway

Books

The Size of Death

Education is a Philosophy

Campus Invocation

Existentialism and the Creative Teacher

Counseling Tips for the Beginning Teacher

Luther For Today

How Love Will Help

Lutheranism and the Educational Ethic

God and I

An Introduction To Theory of Knowledge

The Will in Human Learning

A Dictionary of Philosophical Concepts

PREFACE

This is a dictionary of philosophical concepts. It is not to be looked upon as a dictionary in the usual sense of the term. The definitions of the concepts and, in many instances, their presuppositions, are to be used as analytical descriptors. This means they are to be looked upon as a tool enabling the mind to conceptualize for potentiality. A philosophical concept must never be conceived of as an end in itself. This it never is; rather, it exists to bring ideas and potential thought into existence. Concepts learn from concepts. This is the way in which the mind learns. The philosophical concept exists to bring being and its totality into range to be understood, giving it structure and actualizing its meaning. In other words, making its essence realizable by the mind.

To function materially, the mind needs this essence to work upon; whatever the mind encounters, it seeks to understand and develop when the conative component is active. Since it always moves from the known and the most effective known is the philosophical concept, what is provided here is grist for the inquiring mind.

In a sense, this dictionary is an outgrowth of two of my books in the field of epistemology. In these works, I was forced constantly to define and re-define the concepts with which I was working. While I always decided upon and used a particular definition of a concept, it soon became apparent that other philosophical directions could be pursued as well.

Thought makes further thought possible. Ideas grow, feeding on themselves and other ideas. They also provide sustenance for yet other ideas. The degree to which they can be developed is dependent upon the richness of the essence of the concept at a particular point in time. To offer you a starting point is the purpose of this dictionary.

Russell A. Peterson

THE DICTIONARY

A

Absolute.

An absolute is indivisible, a totality, and the embodiment of infinite thought.

Presuppositions:
1. An absolute is a quality of cause.
2. To conceptualize the absolute is to actualize reality.
3. An absolute is dependent upon nothing other than self-created laws.
4. Only in experience is the learner able to actualize an absolute.
5. To experience the absolute is to possess an idea of its potentiality by means of the material of knowledge.
6. The absolute and the whole serve as cause in the delineation of purpose.
7. To realize the absolute is to actualize the meaningfulness of the absolute.
8. The absolute has as one of its characteristics the teleological principle.
9. The absolute and truth are identical; error is not a characteristic of either concept.
10. An absolute, in its ultimate nature, is mental.
11. The value condition is objective in nature; to comprehend an absolute is to objectify its nature.

Abstract.

To abstract is to expand one's cognitive powers, and move from the concreteness of reality to its implicative values; it is to realize detail in cause and unite parts with a whole.

Abstraction.

Abstraction is the most significant function of method.

Presuppositions:

1. To structure a meaningful future for the learner is the purpose of the process of abstraction.
2. Abstractions evolve from reality; to actualize an abstraction is to determine essence.

Achieve.

To achieve is to fulfill the purpose inherent in the process designed by the means-end relationship.

Acquaintance.

Acquaintance is a severely limited force (in nature) of knowledge. It does not possess the scope nor the purpose of knowledge, or does it involve itself with the integral relationships demanded by knowledge. Acquaintance is limited by its recognition of a thing or thought as only one part of a whole.

Act.

Inherent within act is the potentiality for the determination of direction in finding ends; every act functions as a universal.

Presuppositions:

1. An act, structured by the means-end relationship, is a resultant achieved by means of criteria determined by the value judgment.
2. To determine the nature of a cognitive act it is necessary to discover the degree of intention inherent in its perspective; it is the decision to function through the process of conceptualization.
3. In every cognitive act there is an encounter stemming from the confrontation between subject and object.

4. Imagination is the source of motivation in the creative act.
5. The creative act, in order to finalize its perspective, is dependent upon the potential inherent in the natural law.
6. The intuitive act which supplies meaning to insight is the true proposition.
7. Every act, the conditions of which bring it into existence, is an event structured by law.
8. Presupposed in every act is a meaningful sequence of thought.
9. An act or event cannot exist in isolation; it must possess purpose to exist.
10. To validate an act is to determine its integrity.

Action.

The concept of principle is sterile without a relational dependency upon the perspective of act. The perspective of act is dependent upon need to supply learning momentum.

Presuppositions:
1. False actions evolve from false beliefs.
2. The function of all action is factual unity.

Activity.

An activity, as process, must be dynamic in essence to maintain movement.

Presupposition:
1. Scientific activity pivots about the problem under investigation; the nature of this activity provides the directives which characterize its purpose.

Actuality.

Actuality implies existence. There is the need to realize the implications of the probable and the improbable as these relate to the nature of the existent being or subject. The probable or possible exists when that which is actual has fully realized its own effectiveness as a causative factor in learning. The realm of the possible is impossible without actuality.

Actualization.

Actualization is constant movement; it implies change as process.

Presuppositions:

1. Actualization becomes a resultant through self-realization. It is finite in nature and, as a developer, served the fact in its process of becoming real.
2. Actualization implies a self-realizing process, the essence of which includes the condition out of which reality can be determined.

Adequacy.

An hypothesis aims at description. Adequacy is the resultant factor in description which becomes a power suggesting fulfillment of purpose. Fulfillment implies that the fact under scrutiny is being described through an analysis of the nature, scope and purpose of its substance.

Aim.

Aim is direction; it suggests movement toward the attainment of a goal within which movement and measurement becomes possible through the actualization of propositions.

Alternatives.

A statement of alternatives implies the need for a decision; each alternative provides a setting of other possibilities, describing each and suggesting differences as well as similarities of content and structure inherent in each.

Analogy.

Analogy is a necessity in determining method for argument; it calls for the recognition of resemblances between relationships of contexts rather than between things looked upon as entities.

Presupposition:
1. The use of analogy is meaningless unless it includes an understanding of differences.

Analysis.

Analysis, the aim of knowledge, requires the keen insight proffered in perception for the purpose of abstracting the potential of data.

Presuppositions:
1. To determine potentiality in a value condition is to take the first step in the process of dialectical analysis.
2. In the methodology of analysis, each teleological factor demands movement from theory to verification of truth.
3. The product of analysis is not a resultant which is independent of its process.

Analytic.

There is a dependency factor present in the relationship between the analytic and the synthetic. The one cannot be defined in isolation from the other.

Antecedents.

Antecedents produce value truths which, in turn, suggest purposive action which may result in a consequence which can be understood only through its relationship with its origin.

Anticipation.

The emotive factor is an implicative tenet of the intellect; to anticipate is to move from the emotive to the intellective level of cognitive ability.

Antithesis.

Antithesis concerns itself only with the contexts of a proposition; to bring antithesis into being, the ideas in the proposition will have already been methodically evaluated and their content analyzed.

Appearance.

Appearance and what it projects suggests principles for the analysis of its form and content.

Presuppositions:

1. All being possesses a characteristic structure; inherent within structure is substance; appearance is form designed by the identification of the nature of substance with that of its limiting structure.
2. It is cause alone which permits appearance to serve in the capacity of truth.

Apperception.

The aim of intuition is to develop the intellectual power of apperception; apperception is achieved when the learner is able to provide connective links between seemingly unrelated data.

Application, conceptual.

Conceptual application in the initial stages is always hypothetical.

Appraisal.

Appraisal implies that a search for meaning has been undertaken, and that, within this search, is the endeavor to harmonize the seemingly non-integrative factors which might distort meaning, thereby bringing into existence an understanding of all active agents which have as their responsibility the promulgation of truth.

Apprehension.

Apprehension focuses its attention upon object and not subject;

only in the object will the determinative quality for understanding be found.

Approximate, to.

To approximate is to think abstractly.

Arbitrary.

The learner, when faced with an arbitrary situation, is in turn faced with the problems inherent in factor analysis. Thus, it carries the need to decide which factors are relevant and which factors are not relevant to the subject under study.

Art.

Art implies that a methodology underlies its process of unfolding the constructive idea basic to the creative element within its nature.

Presupposition:

1. An art is dependent upon the effective activity of the mind; this action stimulates what has already been creatively expressed in the texture of a whole.

Assent.

Assent should be given when each segment of a proposition has been examined and proven valid, thereby positing the assurance that a truth has been revealed.

Assertion.

An assertion serves to actuate the question inherent in every proposition. To proffer an assertion is to make a value judgment.

Association.

Association demands of the learner that he identify himself completely with the ideas with which he is working.

Presupposition:

1. Association is only one factor characteristic of relationships; to associate one fact with another is no assurance that knowledge has been gained.

Assumption, perceptual.

An assumption is a value condition, dependent upon the science of judgment to validate its meaningfulness. Because of empirical strains in all methodology, choice remains a characteristic of all perceptual assumptions.

Presupposition:

1. Ontological assumptions are present in every principle of induction.

Attitude.

Every attitude is the result of value condition.

Presuppositions:

1. Science finds its values in the attitudes it engenders. While science demands objectivation for its methodology, it realizes that such demands are unacceptable for the areas of applicability of its results when seen against the needs of man and society.
2. The speculative mind evolves from the process of contemplation; it is the speculative attitude which readies the mind to perceive.

Attributes.

Attributes comprise the essence of the material of knowledge.

Authenticity.

Authenticity is determined by the process of thought and validated by the directives emanating from proven facts.

Awareness.

Awareness is the recognition of the difference between knowledge of and/or knowledge about an object; it implies the possession of the material of knowledge.

Presuppositions:
1. Inherent in the becoming of awareness is the objective trait of intention.
2. The essence of awareness constitutes reality.
3. In the process of intellection, awareness of the relation between parts, and parts with a whole, makes it cognitively possible to analyze the principles which make the relationships meaningful.
4. Awareness implies reflection, the method of which is gained by way of the learning process; self-awareness implies that the process is directed toward the self.
5. Awareness requires a subjective freedom in order to develop its objective trait of intention.

Axiology.

Axiology provides the learner with the opportunity to examine assumptions and postulates; from these, axioms, tautological in nature, structure a terminology suggesting a system of semantics conducive to the development of a language of values.

B

Beauty.

Beauty creates its own value system; as such, it is not passively conceived.

Becoming.

Becoming is both process and fact; it is fact on the move toward self-realization, accomplished when it finds its creative self-propagating ideas in relation to existents. As a process, becoming is identified with the structure (form and content) of the material of knowledge.

Beginnings.

Beginnings suggest the *instant* when cause fulfills itself in purpose. Beginnings ignore the need for fixity because this is not indicative of *Being* in the created order.

Being.

Being is what is known; it is caused, and is the resultant (and yet a process) of the logic of thought. This means:

1. Being is synonymous with itself; being is dependent upon being for its essence.
2. Being reveals itself in cognitive form.
3. Being is real because it can be known.
4. Being alone explains cause.
5. Inherent in the process of cognition is the presupposition of being.
6. Differences in being are possible only between the finite and the infinite.
7. Being is never an end in itself.
8. A basic characteristic of essence in being is rationality.
9. Ideas learn from ideas; ideas are dependent upon facts to realize the meaningfulness of their being. Being is a dependency factor in determining the relationship between existence and essence.
10. To interpret being is to be aware of the implicative values in time.
11. Being makes it possible for metaphysics to function.

12. Being is the unification and integration by the mind of form and matter.
13. The nature of being is determined when the object of learning is experienced. To determine the nature of being is to actualize the metaphysical presuppositions of existence.
14. To discern potentiality in being is to apprehend the differential between degrees of knowledge; it is the object of intuition.
15. Being actualizes itself in purpose.
16. Being is reducible only by means of the systematization of its parts.
17. Being, in the mind of science, is a dependent factor, never isolated, and functions only in relation to a referent.
18. Implied within the structure of being is a totality which bespeaks a power of transcendence.
19. To abstract being is a necessary postulate of knowledge.
20. To actualize being is to presuppose its existence; it is to experience it metaphysically.
21. To experience being is to have related particulars to what is universal.
22. To know being, the mind actualizes its own potential.
23. Being and value are based on identical presuppositions.

Belief.

To believe is to destroy all lines of demarcation between theory, knowledge, and reality. Belief confronts the learner with the reality of such presuppositions as:

1. Belief cannot be distinguished from cause.
2. Belief is a correlative of fact.
3. To determine the logical basis of a belief is to experience its source of derivation. Thus, the basis of all belief is an experienced value.
4. The nature of belief is cognitive.

5. The source of belief is another validated belief.
6. To have identified with truth is to have established a belief. Belief is a participation in truth.
7. The value condition of belief is its presuppositions. To believe is to have found meaning in an existent.

Bias.

Bias accepts itself as an existing part of all learning. In the learner's search for truth, it is bias which suggests that truth does not exist for its own sake. Consequently, to understand the many ramifications and implications of the tenets of truth, bias suggests to itself the need to understand its own strengths and limitations in the handling of truth.

C

Categories.

Categories are abstractions of method.

Presuppositions:

1. Categories become axiomatic when realized in experience.
2. Categories make it possible for explanation to develop its process of analysis.
3. Categories become formative with their new responsibility as postulates.
4. In order for categories to serve as means in experience, they must possess essence.
5. When categories become postulates, they function axiomatically.
6. All categories are intrinsic to reason.
7. Categories evolve by means of the reflective process; in this way they are subject to change.

Category.

The functional purpose of the category is to become a postulate.

Causality.

Causality of matter is efficient causality.

Presuppositions:

1. Causality is based wholly on natural law; natural law evolves from the absolute.
2. Evolving from the laws of causality are new assumptions, all of which depend upon the laws of certainty in the determination of purpose.
3. Causality implies existence.
4. Inherent within the causal law is its own source of power for the generation of the potential.
5. There is no distinction between causality and its laws of operation.
6. Causality is the character of nature.
7. Causality proffers probability as the first step in determining its working principles and defining its laws.
8. Implicit within the nature of cause is the first resultant, that of sequence.
9. Causality is dependent upon the value condition for the justification of its perspective.

Causation.

In causation, reason is synonymous with the event, and dependent upon the connectives inherent in quality and substance.

Cause.

Cause is the embodiment of a tautology, the means of creation.

Presuppositions:

1. Inherent within cause are absolutes with pragmatic natures.

2. Because of the analytical character of cause, one of the most important criteria in validating its law is that of necessity.
3. Cause is force activated by purpose.
4. The concept of cause implies the need for self-fulfillment.
5. Each cause is conditional; without condition, cause cannot exist. The condition of effect is its cause. Cause is the condition of existence.
6. To determine cause or effect it is necessary to start with the assumption that both cause and effect are facts in the material of knowledge. Cause communicates the potentiality of reality to effect.
7. Cause is dependent upon its efficiency components to provide it with relevancy for the human mind.
8. Cause is inherent in each existent; reason for existence is therefore found in essence.
9. Cause is an integral part of the empirical construct of every existent.
10. First cause is independent of the time order.
11. Inherent within every cause are the instrumentalities necessary for the actuation of effect.
12. What is causally possible is logically possible.
13. Cause implies movement.
14. Cause presupposes a system of natural law.
15. To explain the essence of cause is to have realized its developmental nature as an effect. The nature of cause is reflected in effect.
16. Cause implies necessity.
17. Cause must be identified with all numerical harmonies.
18. Inherent within cause is order.
19. Original or just cause leaves room in every construct for the exception.
20. Cause relates particulars.
21. Inherent within cause is perspective; arising from the

antecedent is the potentiality for an event or proposition.
22. Cause is the ground of every presupposition.
23. To actuate the promise of cause is to develop the idea of cause.
24. Cause functions by means of its purpose; moreover, it is transmitted through purpose.
25. A finding of truth always includes the realization of cause.
26. Out of cause arises the potentiality of sequence; sequence is a resultant of cause, never the cause itself
27. To cause is to expand the dimensions of reality.
28. To determine cause is to determine the design inherent in the structure of the rational process.
29. To know cause is to validate its effect.
30. To observe cause, the power of observation requires the perceptive ability of the mind.
31. From cause evolves traits of existence related by associative qualities.
32. The will of cause serves as the generator of regulative laws motivating the development of purpose in data.

Certainty.

The goal of the probable is certainty. Since conditions undergird the probable, certainty is not reached until each condition is weighed and compared against other conditions and this relationship emanating from the two is positive.

Certitude.

Certitude is an act of faith in the material of knowledge. Certitude requires no research and observation is unnecessary.

Chance.

Chance is an inherent possibility found within any opportunity for discovery of the unknown.

Change.

Change implies movement which in itself is conditioned by what is relative in purpose; it implies a process which is continuous by nature.

Presuppositions:

1. In change, the process of becoming is realized in the function of the content of knowledge.
2. Change cannot occur without cause.
3. Change is dependent upon the constancy of its correlatives for its movement.
4. Change never occurs in isolation; it is divisible.
5. In change, substance functions to establish new relationships in essence.
6. Every change implies the fusion of the old with the new; the identity of the old is lost; the new is a blend of the two.
7. In every change, the law which governs movement reflects cause.
8. Change is a characteristic of reality.
9. Change is universal in nature, scope, and purpose.

Character.

Character suggests the use of wholes; within the whole is a unity comprised of particulars. Character is understood as character when the assumptions pertaining to particulars are strengthening the relationship between the corresponding postulates.

Choice.

Choice is a matter between means and ends.

Presuppositions:

1. Choice must evolve from the nature of the existent to be explained.
2. Choice is justified in terms of means employed and ends satisfied.

3. Choice is an integral part of every methodology.
4. Choice operates on the working base of value.

Circumstantial.

The circumstantial may not express the causal in research. When the source or cause has been determined the circumstantial becomes meaningless.

Claim, cognitive.

Cognitive claims are descriptive.

Clarification.

Clarification means that a point of reference has been validated as being exact and relevant and all irrelevancies have been removed from the factual setting.

Clarify, to.

To clarify is an inherent demand of means and end; clarification is attributable to the means-end relationship.

Classes.

Classes refer to things not considered entities within themselves; there is a similarity between these things because of the existing connectives expressing a relational status.

Classification.

Classification evolves from conclusions drawn when observation has led the learner to weigh all facts under consideration.

Cognition.

Cognition is the process of knowing.

Presuppositions:
1. Cognition provides meaning to activity.
2. All cognition is based upon criteria evolving from method.

3. Cognition orders experience.
4. Cognition projects the use of hypotheses in the learning process.
5. Cognition determines whether or not order is present in experience.
6. A cognition is a proposition since it is a condition for further learning.
7. Cognition opens reality to the mind.
8. It is the process of cognition which enables the individual to transcend himself.

Coherence, experience.

Coherence is determined when its implicative values become synonymous with experience. To determine coherence is to synthesize validated goals.

Comparison.

To compare is to determine the relevancy of postulates used consistently in any formula.

Presupposition:

1. As the mind functions, it compares comparisons.

Communication.

To communicate is to determine the intrinsic character of perception.

Comparability.

Comparability is the functional principle governing the applicability of the scientific method.

Completeness.

Completeness uses a base which might be labeled as considerations. Considerations suggest the need for an integration of variations. To be complete is a means whereby its purposive nature is realized in its service.

Completion.

A basic tenet in the Law of Being in nature is completion. Completion is the fulfillment of purpose.

Comprehension.

Every facet of learning is an integral part of the whole; each has its particular place within the framework of this same whole. Comprehension, as an integrating process, is the ability to see the fact in its proper place and within the context of its legitimate relationships.

Presupposition:

1. To objectify levels of comprehension requires levels of belief.

Conation.

Conation is a value concept, the resultant of the learner's quest for purpose and goals. Conation recognizes the presence of particularized connectives in each goal as the goal evolves from definitive schemata.

Concept.

While every concept is the result of abstraction, it is the concept alone which translates the ideal into the real. The concept is the essence of thought, an expression of human sensibility.

Presuppositions:

1. To apply a concept is to have determined its degree of openness.
2. Determinants of the concept are found in every fact.
3. The concept is the most important guide in experimentation.
4. It is the concept which determines the validity of a hypothesis.
5. Within the structure of the concept is the synthetic quality of value; it is value which permits the concept to analyze and

determine the potentiality of an idea.
6. The meaning of a concept is dependent upon the qualities of its essence.
7. The concept is organically related to particulars and transcends them.
8. Without purpose, the concept is sterile in nature.
9. The essence of the concept is spiritual.
10. The concept has within its own structure the point of origin and ends.
11. To define a concept is to determine the degree of abstraction necessary for the analysis of the concept.
12. To validate a concept through its assumptions in order to determine consistency of nature is to place logic and reality on the same plane of existence.
13. The true concept is a literal copy of nature.

Conceptions, meaningfulness.

Conceptions are meaningful only at the perceptual level.

Conceptualization.

The homologication of relationships is the aim of the process of conceptualization.

Presuppositions:
1. To function through conceptualization is to increase the minds ability for prediction.
2. For the learner to conceptualize is to transcend the limits of the construct inherent in each datum and replace the idea of an entity with the idea of organism.
3. To conceptualize is to work with universals alone; only the universal suggests the ideal.

Conceptualize, to.

The ability to conceptualize is dependent upon the potentiality of theory; it is to experience the potential of a proposition and apprehend a degree of truth.

Conclusion, premise.

To validate a conclusion is to have determined the truth of the premise. To *know* a conclusion is to *know* its premise.

Conclusion, validation.

To validate a conclusion, the mind accepts the assumptions and affirms the consequences.

Conclusions.

Conclusions are inherent in every premise.

Presuppositions:

1. Implicit conclusions are inherent in any tacit assumption.
2. Conclusions are validated only when premises have been subjected to the same tests.

Concrete.

The concrete deals in relationships between details of fact, existents, and the structure of the probable.

Condition.

Condition has a character; inherent in its nature is the need to explain itself as an integral part of causality. The condition of an existent implies the "why" of existence.

Presuppositions:

1. To determine the connectives between a succession of becomings is to understand the function of the value condition.
2. Each value condition abstracts causality.
3. Inherent within the value condition is the cognitive value.
4. Condition alone does not determine the results of

experimentation; it is the teleologically conditioned perspective in the material truth which possesses this ability.
5. Values are meaningful only in relationships; relativism pertains only to the externals realized as such in these relationships; relativity then is one construct of every value condition.
6. To change a condition is to recognize the potential of law.
7. The value condition posits the fact whether or not something is true or false.
8. Conditions reflect their meaning only in relation to the events or occurrences which evolve from them.
9. Control of conditions relevant to possessing an understanding of a problem implies the use of limitations; these limitations strengthen the whole until its parts (or conditions) are conceived as wholes.
10. Conditions presuppose the relevancy of purpose; to fulfill purpose, ascertained facts supply the knowledge necessary for attainment of specified ends.
11. Factors relevant to understanding the setting of a problem permit the desired potential purposive action to become actualized.

Conduct, moral.

Basic to an understanding of the responsibility of moral conduct is the inherent responsibility of causality.

Conjecture.

Through the process of conjecture, the learner is enabled to analyze each hypothesis and determine its relevancy to the problem, as well as its relational implications to other hypotheses which proffer themselves for consideration.

Connectives.

Relations are synthetic in nature; to achieve the object of

experimentation is to determine the nature of the connectives inherent in material truth. A synthetic bias is always characteristic of a connective. Synthesis provides the connective with a perspective for delineation.

Connectives, knowledge.

The connectives between fields in the material of knowledge are operational; to learn, the mind must experience the relationships.

Connectors.

Connectors essentially serve as the essence between the cause and its effect.

Consciousness.

Consciousness is innately selective.

Presuppositions:
1. Consciousness is measured for depth by degrees.
2. Consciousness is an awareness of the meaningfulness of an existent.
3. Consciousness implies movement.
4. Consciousness is perception in the act of functioning.
5. Consciousness is dependent upon potentiality for its depth.
6. Reflective consciousness implies that use has been made a chain of implications.
7. Consciousness implies the use of relationships to determine the presence of representation in the subject-object dichotomy.
8. Consciousness rises from the creative process, a recognition then, of its need to constantly transcend itself.
9. Consciousness is always structured.
10. Consciousness is analogous to value.

Consequence.

Consequence is dependent upon conclusion; only in this way is the mind able to validate a conclusion.

Considerations, rhetorical.

Inherent within the process of argument are the directions taken by propositions; rhetorical considerations span the diverse arguments and serve as the connective link unifying the arguments presented.

Consistency.

Consistency, while it suggests the presence of truth, is but a condition of an existent.

Constants.

Constants are referred to as such only when the relationship between causal factors is clearly understood.

Construct, scientific.

Experience, to realize itself, actualizes meaning; meaning is explanatory in nature evolving from the process of deduction thereby providing a scientific construct with a condition for its value judgment.

Constructs.

While entities are not real but inferred, constructs provide entities with form.

Contemplation.

In contemplation, every object is considered in relation to a whole.

Content.

Form presupposes matter or content; content provides form with value.

Context.

Context implies relationships; such relationships categorize perspective in methodology in terms of results.

Context, cognitive.

The cognitive context is dependent upon the learner's recognition of the fact that universals are comprised of particulars.

Continuity.

For existence, continuity relies on a relationship which identifies dependent factors found within causation.

Contradiction.

Contradiction is not to be found in the nature of an existent, but rather, in the mind of the process of knowing. In every law of contradiction, the change which is necessary reflects cause.

Control.

To control is to limit the attitudes and reactions of the learner to evidence factualized and applied to the problem under consideration.

Coordination.

Coordination is the actualization of seemingly invariant factors, uniting them into a harmonious functionary for the use of facts.

Correlation.

Correlation is a process wherein relevant data is structured in order to compare differences in findings.

Correspondence.

Correspondence suggests the need for the learner to identify the purpose of the whole and relate his findings with the purpose of the parts.

Corroboration.

Corroboration is the method employed in validating factual material.

Create, to.

To create is to expand order in cause and discover value.

Creation.

Creation is developed by imagination and excited by the potential. Creation is a projection of the real but transcends it; an image, newly structured, is determined by the idea being defined by means of its power of extension.

Presuppositions:

1. The creative laws of creation can be known qualitatively as well as quantitatively.
2. Because all of creation is dialectical, its universals as well as its particulars are discoverable.
3. Creation is growth and development; both growth and development imply preconceived direction — for one reason alone, the determination of potentiality.
4. Creation is the act of existence.
5. Creation is organic development.
6. The process of creation is dependent upon the unity found in order to give it direction.

Creative, to be.

To be creative is to give birth to two ideas, both of which are seen not as entities but in terms of their dependency factors; in creativity lies the genesis of totality. To be truly creative, the learner must be aware of all implications of his bias.

Creativity, evolution.

Creativity evolves from an actualization process which is dependent upon the ability of one idea to learn from another idea.

Presuppositions:

1. The metaphysical connective between creativity and

spontaneity is the imagination.
2. All creativity presupposes constant thought.
3. Vision is the pivot of creativity.

Crisis.

A crisis presupposes the existence of differences; crises arise with the failure to evaluate value perspectives.

Criteria.

Criteria, concerned with conditions based on assumptions, determine the validity of the relationship between the ideal and its corresponding value.

Criticism.

Criticism transcends mere inquiry; it follows examination and evaluation and bases its applicative projection on the adequacy of expression.

Culture.

Culture is a resultant, the embodiment of a synthesized system of values and ideas arising from within the relationship between man and his society.

Curiosity.

Curiosity is indicative of the unsatisfied mind; the unsatisfied mind has been unable to reach an understanding of the problem under consideration or follow the implications emanating from relationships surrounding the problem.

D

Data.

Data is actualized, not as object but as product, by means of the process of analytical discovery and description.

Presuppositions:
1. To become meaningful, all data requires interpretation.
2. The mind functions by means of, and through, data. Thus, data is not the object of thought.
3. Existence justifies the recognition of observable data as the essence of the material of knowledge; for the mind to interpret it as particulars in the realm of being is to have validated its essence by the cognitive process.
4. Perceptual data is selective in nature, scope and purpose; it is dependent upon *a priori* knowledge to give it relevancy.
5. To discern potential in data is to ascertain the nature of the subject of cognition.
6. To function abstractly, the process of intellection requires data to serve as the source of analysis.

Datum.

Datum is what *is* to actualize its reality is to discover its introspective nature.

Presupposition:
1. Datum serves as the discriminator of analysis and its processes.

Decision.

Decision implies that use has been made of alternatives; since alternatives bespeak an enduring ontology, decision is reached only within the perspective which has its setting in a freedom of intellectual curiosity and inquiry.

Presuppositions:
1. The function of decision is to act.
2. The human decision is dependent upon attitude to determine the maturity of its judgment.

Define, to.

To define is to explain the logical structure of concepts and explain their meaning.

Definition.

A definition is born a proposition and functions to reveal the material of essence.

Presuppositions:

1. Experience alone confirms a definition.
2. A definition expresses the assertive qualities of a decision.
3. Definition actualizes the material of knowledge.
4. Predictive meaning is found in every definition.
5. Definitions, to be meaningful, depend upon the ability of the mind for conceptualization.
6. All definitions are propositions because they are decisions.

Describe, to.

To describe is to have judged by determining the validity of the referent used in the frame of reference.

Description.

Description creates the problematic setting.

Presuppositions:

1. The methodology employed in description is empirically based; this is a presupposition of every law of logic.
2. To describe is to judge the essence of experience.
3. The ability to describe is dependent upon the ability to interpret.
4. To describe, the learner must become an integral part of the process of description.

Design, teleology.

The teleology of design is dependent upon the organismic perspective of its construct in determining its ultimate principles. These principles are metaphysical in nature and scope. Visual design contains within its limitations, an organization of parts.

Diagnosis.

Diagnosis is an examination of new factors and claims which vary from the adequacy of established norms.

Dialectic.

To determine its potentiality, the dialectic periodically returns to its cause.

Presuppositions:

1. Intuition and experience constitute the essence of the dialectic.
2. The dialectic evolves from the hypothesis in the process of being validated.

Difference.

The transparency characteristics of difference implies an awareness of internal structural relationships. Difference is the outstanding characteristic of an occurrence.

Differences.

Differences imply levels of quality; quality suggests similarities of origin; equated differences are verifiable only on the basis of similarities.

Differentiation.

Differentiation is an ontological determinate.

Presupposition:

1. The control of differentiation lies solely in methodology.

Direction.

Direction is teleologically determined; it is inherent in every category.

Presuppositions:
1. Direction is inherent in all experience.
2. Direction is inherent in every proposition; knowledge is acquired by means of this direction; direction evolves from insight received through awareness.
3. In determining direction via the hypothesis in the scientific method, the learner must validate the idea before moving on to experimentation.

Disciplines.

By their very nature, disciplines design and structure foundations of concepts.

Discover, to.

To discover is to determine potentiality.

Discovery.

A discovery is a stepping stone to discovery.

Presuppositions:
1. Belief is a basic ingredient of any hypothesis; to discover is to believe in the possible.
2. Existence challenges; discovery is the acceptance of challenge.
3. To discover is to create.
4. The spirit of discovery and expression lies in their presentment.
5. Discovery is always the result of empirically oriented method.
6. Discovery is a process.

Distinctions.

Distinctions are made only by means of analysis; categories arise from distinctions.

Distinctness.

Divisibility is characteristic of the whole; divisibility suggests the need to dissect the whole, to understand the relationship, therefore the distinctions of the parts.

Diversification.

The capacity for diversification resides only in the mind.

Dogmatism.

Dogmatism remains ill-defined when its purpose is directed to the yet unknown; dogmatism, rightly defined, suggests the need to subject the material of an object to the type of methodology, the procedure of which will reveal cognitive meaning, therefore, fact.

Doubt.

Doubt fosters a deliberateness of purpose. Its purpose is to destroy itself.

This is done by cultivating a sense of question and suspicion in the mind of the learner. Question and suspicion of unproved data prompts the need for verification, consequently, clarification of all facets of the implications of the object of the study.

Duality.

Duality implies dependence of all aspects of the learning process upon one another. Scientific knowledge must lean heavily upon theory; theoretical knowledge must lean heavily upon the scientific method.

Duration.

Duration, the existence of which is for the purpose of valuation, is one construct identifiable in every element within the material of the created order.

E

Eclecticism.

Eclecticism is the resultant of the integration of seemingly unrelated and independent facets of being, providing the abstractions necessary for the uniting of the basic intelligence of each being within its whole.

Education.

Education is the process of designing a schema of intradisciplines for the purpose of best utilizing the many facets of experience.

Presuppositions:

1. All philosophies of education, as philosophies of learning, are reductive of the material of knowledge.
2. The function of a philosophy of education is to determine the nature of both means and ends, and do so by designing the proper method for such realization.
3. Education rests upon metaphysical postulates which can be actualized only by an empirically oriented methodology.

Effect.

Effect is never static; it is a process implying movement in becoming.

Presuppositions:

1. Antecedent to every effect is cause.
2. It is through an effect the learner recognizes design in harmony.
3. Effect, after evolving from cause, can serve as initiator of movement.
4. Effect is the realization of the potential; herein is the

influence inherent in the potential realized and consequently verified.

5. Spontaneity is the characteristic of effect which assures the mind that actuation has proceeded from cause.

Efficiency.

Efficiency implies that order within sequence of events has been achieved.

Presupposition:

1. While observation and experimentation characterize method, arising from the procedural base is the need for efficiency; this is determined by the theoretical synthesis of observation and experimentation making it possible for creativity to exert itself.

Elementary.

That which is elementary in nature possesses reason for being and serves to develop advanced principles emanating from the first cause, expressing itself through primary connotations.

Elements.

Elements essentially are parts of wholes and characterized by wholes, the characteristics of which are inherent in the parts.

Elimination.

Elimination is a self-perpetuating process; it carries within itself a system of rejection directed toward the disproved.

Emotive, power.

The power of the emotive in any facet of epistemology is dependent upon the ability of the mind for visualization.

Empirically, to create.

To create empirically is to think imaginatively.

Empiricism.

Empiricism is the means by which knowledge and its material is explained.

Presuppositions:
1. While empiricism bases its own structure of content on experiential reaction, this does not imply an exclusion of transcendental factors from being recognized for their influence upon experience itself.
2. Empiricism is concerned with the revelatory powers of the material of knowledge; it provides the setting in which the learning process can function.
3. Facts in relation to facts demand a process of technique for self-actualization. This process is empirical in nature and its purpose is to epistemologically serve fact.
4. In order for empiricism to maintain its stance as a process, its basic methodology must always retain the quality of self-correction.
5. Empiricism is a purposive process used to interpret sequence in the development of propositions.
6. Empiricism is self-correcting.

Encompassing.

Each proposition basically finds its setting in Being. To encompass means is to surround each proposition with ideas and use the process of thought to analyze the being of the proposition before consideration is given to parts or implications.

End.

To evaluate the meaningfulness of end in its relation to means, the referent for both is the degree of knowledge attained and used for their definition.

Presuppositions:

1. To determine (the realization of) end is to have recognized an instrumentation for the fulfillment of purpose; thus, there has been the awareness of means and the part it played in reaching end.
2. To determine the potentiality inherent in each end is to reduce it by teleological means; this implies that even end is a process of consciousness.
3. To clarify purpose in an end is to have found meaning in its intention and relevancy in its nature.
4. In considering means as "ways" to an end and evaluate this instrumentation of methodology, the end must be defined in light of the teleological principle inherent in means.

Ends.

Ends remain a process of change; thus, an object is an integral part of means.

Presuppositions:

1. Ends are cognitive in function.
2. Ends are organismic in nature, scope and purpose. Thus, they are dependent upon the past for meaning and actualize themselves though means.
3. It is impossible to define ends without determining the degree of truth inherent in the means.
4. Ends must be validated by the means employed.
5. Ends imply the use of means; therefore, a number of *ways* are suggested via possibilities.
6. Ends must be postulated by the will if there is to be intention.

Energy.

Energy is the source of motivation; motivation serves to structure a setting for motion, thereby limiting its activity.

Enjoyment.

Enjoyment is determined by its inherent value system and based upon a relationship between a goal and its object.

Entities.

Entities exist only as mental tenets; the creative process of intellection destroys these tenets when the value condition is actualized.

Presuppositions:
1. Whatever exists is functional in nature; therefore entities even as ideas are not real; they do not possess functional purpose.
2. Entities become ideas when existence and essence are recognized as Being. To experience Being is to recognize that entities do not exist.

Entity, actual.

The actual aspect of the entity implies that the possible has been attained, brought into being and realized. It is the fulfillment of becoming insofar as cause has been effected and now serves as a stimulant to process.

Environment.

Since totality is an integral part of the functional responsibility of the mind, environment provides the setting in which totality can be perceived.

Epistemology.

Epistemology is a determinant; the purpose of epistemology is discovery; discovery is the resultant of epistemological determination.

Presuppositions:
1. One assumption in epistemology is the need to be fully aware of the implicative values inherent in metaphysics.
2. Inherent within the mind of epistemology is a methodological construct used to determine rationality in the learning process. This alone guarantees that knowledge is knowledge of reality.
3. The laws of logic determine the experimental values derived from epistemology.
4. The working hypothesis of epistemology is the methodology inherent in ontology.
5. All epistemology is perceptual in nature; this implies a dependency upon the logic of both particulars and universals.
6. The basic problem of epistemology is to determine and justify the working relationships between the inductive and deductive methods. Epistemology functions by means of its theories of perception; in this way is empirical evidence gained which is sufficient to assure epistemological methodology of its operational ground, namely, circularity.
7. To philosophically analyze the material of knowledge is to structure the purpose and responsibility of epistemology.

Err, to.

To err is to believe in and through ignorance.

Error.

Error remains a possibility as related to particulars until the fact of an event or proposition is proven consistently true.

Essence.

Essence is the quality of substance.

Presuppositions:

1. The relationship between quantity and quality and their evaluing correlates is the greatest determinants in the analysis of essence.
2. In essence resides the conditions under which consciousness can function.
3. To determine the validity of an existent as bearing the quality of the present is to recognize continuity of essence.
4. Essence implies the totality of existence inherent within the developmental factors presupposed in its own being.
5. The human mind categorizes essence by means of its structure; existence is assumed in essence.
6. Essence serves as the ground of the process of conceptualization.
7. Quality determines the nature of essence.
8. A spiritual essence is by nature a function of time; it is in a constant state of potentiality.
9. To actuate essence is to determine meaning in existence.
10. While the mind measures, essence, it realizes that to do so objectively it must evaluate the perspective of dimension.

Ethics, nature.

The nature of ethics evolves from the factual base of ethics.

Evaluation.

All evaluation is a movement toward individualization.

Presuppositions:

1. Evaluation, in the final analysis, must concern itself with cause.
2. Since all evaluation is subject to change, it remains relative and reflective.
3. All evaluation is cognitive.

Event.

An event is a cause in motion.

Presuppositions:
1. Every event carries within itself the possibility for its actualization.
2. Every event is conditioned by the effectiveness of its cause.
3. Working alternatives provide the mind with criteria for the determination of validity in the construct of the creative event.
4. Each event is dependent upon antecedent events for continued existence.
5. Inherent within the essence of an event is cause.
6. The form or construct of any event is dependent upon its inherent relationships.
7. An event is a particular in a law.
8. It is the mind which creates the meaningfulness of an event and attributes to its scope.
9. Because an event is a cause in motion, what happens or takes place is always new.
10. Events are related by means of the activity of the mind; that is to say, an event is historical in nature as well as in function.
11. To understand events is to experience their implications.
12. Events exist to imply conditions as well as potentialities.

Evidence.

Evidence is brought into being with the agreement of suppositions as these relate to fact.

Evil.

The active human mind realizes that it must evaluate what it assimilates; evil is that force of being which makes it difficult and at times impossible for the mind to appraise objectively all facets of the item under study. Evil carries within itself the projectile of incompleteness. Evil has succeeded in its task when the mind evaluates without possessing complete data on which to base its appraisal.

Excellence.

Excellence depends upon an obedience to the spiritual components of the laws of logic.

Exist, to.

To exist is to individualize a decision, and do so in terms of a causal relationship.

Existence.

Existence is predicated on choice and the freedom inherent in its process.

Presuppositions:
1. Only thought and its many processes are able to discover the diversity in existence.
2. Existence finds its meaning in the ontological base of essence.
3. To posit the existence of something independent of the act of cognition is to suggest existence without essence.
4. Existence and essence imply as identical cause as well as effect.
5. When defined as being synonymous, existence and essence imply meaning as an object to be realized by the mind.
6. Everything which exists has its ground in being.
7. Existence closes the gap between idea and reality.
8. What exists can be known subjectively.
9. Implied within, and tantamount to, existence is the material of knowledge.
10. What exists, exists in our minds because it exists external to the mind.

11. What exists is actualized by the mind to determine its essence.
12. The quality of an existent is found in its essence.
13. To abstract reality from existence is to destroy its potentiality.
14. What exists must be considered real in all categories.
15. To define existence is to do so in terms of the degrees of truth.
16. To experience existence is to metaphysically experience meaning.
17. To discover traits of existence is to discern objects of knowledge.
18. Existence and truth do not presuppose value because value is inherent in both.
19. To be meaningful, existence is dependent upon its correlative component validity.
20. Existence implies value.
21. Existence is a *what* as well as a *why*.

Existent.

An existent is the integration and unification of all of its attributes.

Presuppositions:

1. An existent is an absolute in relation to its cause.
2. To analyze an existent is to begin with factors which are self-clarifying.
3. An existent *is* because of its conditions of existence.
4. The essence of an existent is historical in nature.
5. Every existent possesses the privilege of extension.
6. Every existent is an expression of a formative idea.
7. Inherent within the structure of an existent are relationships determined by the nature of the existent. In this way, the potential of the existent is realized; this is the basis of all material of knowledge.

8. In every existent, its nature is determined by its qualities.
9. An existent implies the presence of an objective referent.
10. Within every existent are particulars ontologically based in the quality of the relationships engendered.
11. The basic presupposition of every existent is faith.
12. Every existent possesses purpose.
13. Every existent possesses within itself the proof of its own structure.
14. An integral component of every existent is a universal.
15. An existent, as substance, possesses value implications; it is insight into substance rather than existence which determines the conditions of those implications.
16. Categorically, all existents are real regardless of their level of being.

Existentialism, infinity.

Existentialism affirms infinity.

Expectation.

Expectation, as a concept, has been structured by the mind via its ability for conceptualization.

Experience.

Experience expresses the degree of apprehension envisioned in reality; it determines the functional relationship among abstractions.

Presuppositions:
1. Experience is synonymous with the acquisition of knowledge.
2. Theory is a process of intellection by means of which experience is actualized through meaning.
3. The *a priori* factor in experience evolves from the form as well as the substance of the proposition.
4. Experience is the process of causation.

5. Experience is the unifier of relationships.
6. Experience is the process of awareness.
7. A basic ingredient in experience is the teleological factor of awareness.
8. The value condition is the base of all experience.
9. To experience is to modify behavior.
10. Experience validates the category and thereby enables it to become a postulate.
11. Experience cannot be confined to categories.
12. Experience evolves by means of the process of conceptualization.
13. The context of experience is a relationship of data.
14. Experience integrates and unifies differences.
15. All experience is direct; the implications of this proposition suggest that every cause demands an effect. This is to say that cause implies direction.
16. As the learner experiences, he discovers the ontological character of his object of knowing.
17. Experience implies that at its core of realization, empiricism functions to assure that the process of discovery is one of opening up the potential.
18. It is experience which destroys the concept of entity.
19. Experience is synonymous with event but transcends it in meaning.
20. Experience structures the context for existence.
21. The learner must experience in order to experience; to explain, it is first necessary to experience meaning.
22. Experience alone makes it possible for generalizations to form.
23. Experience is always acting on its newly created hypotheses.
24. Experience is immediate.
25. All experience is inferential in the same way an idea

requires the use of a referent.
26. The learner experiences experience.
27. Logic and its methodology is implicit in experience.
28. To gain meaning is to experience.
29. Learning is experiential; experience implies that the means-end relationship has functioned by means of its organizational perspective.
30. While experience is a resultant of the methodology inherent in analysis, it is also the cause of method.
31. With the actualization of experience comes the realization of the mind. Experience is identical with the mind's reaction to its meaning.
32. Experience is synthetical in nature; it begins as an analytical process and seeks to realize itself as its own ideal, that of synthesis.
33. Meaning is synonymous with experience; it is experience which provides the objectivity through which methodology can function.
34. Experience is the origin of experience.
35. To experience perceptually is to synthesize meaning in order to structure the value judgment.
36. Inherent within experience is its perspective; the functional base of this perspective is logic.
37. Inherent within the perspective of experience is an awareness of its potentiality for further experience.
38. For experience to actuate itself it must first realize its potentiality as an act.
39. Experience has, as one of its functions, the regulation of presuppositions.
40. Experience connotes an immediacy of stance, recognizing that the primary need of experience is to experience.
41. Experience is the ground from which the problem evolves.
42. All experience is problematic.

43. The quality of an experience is determined by the evolving value judgment.
44. Experience is the revelation of reality. To experience is to participate in reality.
45. The only relational component in experience is the concept.
46. It is the relationships inherent in experience which are of greatest interest to the scientific method.
47. The responsibility of experience is to enable the learner to experience at a more meaningful level.
48. Experience is structured by facts and ideas handled as thought.
49. To determine what experience is like is to experience its implicative values.
50. To develop and expand experience is to more fully conceptualize its value.
51. To interpret experience is to base the method of interpretation on order.
52. To order experience is to understand its potential.
53. To experience is to internalize its concepts.
54. To experience is to make distinctions.
55. To experience experience which is to determine its reality, the mind must formulate a proposition to actualize its meaning.
56. To experience is to identify the material of knowledge and relate the dependent connectives to ontological premises.
57. To experience is to make it possible to experience.
58. To experience is to have moved from the unknown to the known by means of the theoretical premises inherent in the relationship between the mind and the symbols projected by the material of knowledge.
59. To experience is to actualize the real; this is true whether it pertains to an idea or physical matter.
60. To experience is to apprehend truth in greater detail.

61. To experience is to actualize an emerging unity.
62. Experience is dependent upon experience in order to function as a totality in any setting.
63. Every experience possesses value. To experience is to find value; its quality is relational essence, verified by means of its power of creativity. To experience is to have observed, experimented and perceived; that is, being knowledgeable.

Experiment, to.

To experiment is to suggest meaning.

Experimentation.

To experiment is to methodically analyze the known to determine the unknown.

Presuppositions:

1. The essence of an experiment will determine whether or not the results can be reproduced after the process of validation has been completed.
2. Experimentation begins with the known; insight into the known provides the working context for the methodology in experimentation.
3. Experimentation is a process, conditioned by the insights given through controlled observation.
4. The purpose of experimentation is to determine the validity or nonvalidity of an idea.

Explanation.

To explain is to connect ideas with facts.

Presuppositions:

1. Explanation is found only in an existent.
2. Explanation is found only in meaning.
3. To explain implies the establishment of a relationship; explanation is always intrinsic to the implicative values

inherent in meaning.
4. Explanation enlarges the potentiality of fact.
5. To explain is to have determined purpose.
6. To explain is to have fulfilled the function of theory.

Expression.

An expression is the realization of a meaningful satisfication; the psychological impulse generating the expression emanates from a non-satisfactory or controlling statement of intention.

Presupposition:
1. Expressions, like propositions, reveal meaning only by means of their reason for existence.

Extension.

Extension presupposes the existence of substance; material may be extended; thought never. Extension is one of the qualities of substance.

F

Fact.

Every fact implies the existence of another fact; it is conceptual in nature, a partial profile of another fact, and a whole.

Presuppositions:
1. To determine the antecedents of a fact is to determine the nature, scope and purpose of cause.
2. A fact remains a fact as long as the learner knows of its existence and is able to see it in relation to other sources of belief.
3. In every fact is a common denominator; evolving from this denominator are the principles which unite one part with another part, and parts with a whole.

4. The responsibility of the hypothesis is to suggest alternatives; while a fact cannot live if placed in isolation, the conceptualization process makes of fact a conjecture until it can be identified with other facts.
5. To be conscious of a validated fact is to be aware of its implicative values, suggesting an implicit consistency with a whole.
6. Conditions antecedent to representation permit the mind to abstract empirical data and form constructs for the purpose of determining correlations between facts.
7. Facts permit a decision to be made.
8. The fact is the determiner of truth.
9. Facts learn from facts; this is done by means of the theoretical base of the inherent relationships.
10. When a fact functions as a fact it provides generalizations; from these generalizations arise opportunities for the mind to synthesize and interpret newly discovered facts.
11. The functional principle underlying the structure of every fact is the directive emanating from the inferential perspective.
12. Each fact exists in a historical setting; inherent within the fact, then, is a part which permits it to become actualized when seen in relation to another fact.
13. The fact has meaning only when it probes into human nature.
14. Facts are constructed upon presuppositions; since it is the fact and its structure which is to be explained, the hypothesis serves to open fact, describing both limitations and potentialities. Hypothesis and fact are related in the same way methodology and a resultant are related.
15. When an existent is declared a fact it is within the realm of knowledge and becomes an integral part of its material.
16. To answer the questions evolving from a fact is to possess a

knowledge of the laws undergirding the fact.
17. To learn is to allow the fact to take the learner in and unto itself.
18. When a fact is no longer isolated, and in its relationship to another fact reveals the working principles between the two, the mind begins to retain tenets proffered in the potentiality for learning.
19. The mind of a fact has only one responsibility, that of integration.
20. Every fact (and its working principles) evolves from propositions based on natural law.
21. To experience meaning is to acquire knowledge; to acquire knowledge is to be aware of the nature of a fact. To be aware of the nature of a fact is to have perceived its relational value as a whole.
22. To actualize a fact is to understand the implicative values inherent within the ontological base of that fact.
23. There is a potency in every fact.
24. Facts reveal what *is,* as well as suggest the potentiality of *being.*
25. Facts are realizable only from their principles. The principle underlying facts destroy the limitations of the human mind.
26. Facts and reality are identical.
27. Within the existence of the fact lies its relationship to other facts, determined by the construct of perception and its contingency factors.
28. The significance of a fact is realized only when the fact is transparent to the learner.
29. Each fact is social in nature since it exists as existential knowledge only when it evolves as a value and part of a larger construct.
30. To recognize the potentiality of a fact is to have analyzed its structure. In order to exist, each fact is structured according

to all of the causal relationships with other facts.
31. To actualize a fact is to structure its object and determine the derivative nature of each of its hypotheses.
32. Facts cannot be brought into being unless value judgments are made pertaining to the validity of each, as they stand in juxtaposition.
33. To correlate facts requires the use of the principle of causality.
34. Facts are dependent on other facts for relevancy and meaning. To determine a fact is to determine its relationship to other facts.
35. To experience a fact is to know and validate it.
36. To go beyond fact is to have determined its value.
37. To know a fact is to know its dependent relationships.
38. To validate a fact is to possess the ability to select, from among a number of choices, data which strengthens relationship; it is to understand its own presuppositions.
39. Fact is ultimate only in the sense of its total apprehension by the mind.
40. A fact asserts a fact about values. Fact is the substance of value.

Factuality.

Factuality is present in every working hypothesis; this is not to suggest that factuality is an entity, only that it is functional in nature.

Presupposition:
1. To discover the factuality of a theory is to move from observation to experimentation in the scientific method.

Falsity.

Falsity is that which describes a non-fact or a non-existent.

Feeling.

Feeling is a dominant event out of which value conditions arise; it is for this reason the self image is dependent upon the self knowledge contained in every value judgment.

Figure.

Form and function characterize figure; both form and function comprise parts, all of which are dependent upon the pattern of order for meaning.

Finality.

Finality bespeaks a limitation or fulfillment of purpose; the accepted purpose posits the criterion in determining whether or not the ultimate has been gained.

Findings, scientific.

Scientific findings when first actualized posit the need for the learner to analyze the problem of the existing relationship between what has now been "found" and the historicity of the fact in the larger schemata.

Focus, to determine.

To determine focus is to use the formal components of existence as a basis of operation.

Form.

Form is means, not an end, in the material of knowledge; it is the vision of matter generated by the mind.

Presuppositions:
1. In all cause, form is apparent as one dimension of content.
2. Form and function are always present in the matter, thus realizable in substance.
3. All form is innate in its material.

4. The relationship existing between form and quality is the same as that which exists between existence and essence. Neither are entities, and one cannot exist without the other.

Formulation.

Within the perspective of formulation is the problem situation; since it is a problem, a revision of some sort is in order, the pattern arising from the revision suggests a systematization of relationships for the determination of its solution.

Fortiori, a.

Reason, says the *a fortiori* postulate, has no need of postulates nor self-evident axiology.

Foundation.

To determine points of origination within a totality and recognize the potentiality constitutive of function in fact is to have structured a foundation from which the process of intellection can move.

Freedom.

Freedom implies the presence of purpose. The realization of purpose, regardless of hindering circumstances, suggests that consistency of judgment has provided the setting for stability of movement.

Presuppositions:

1. To transcend means that the meaning of freedom has been realized.
2. Truth maintains its transparency only when complete freedom is attained.

Fulfill, to.

To fulfill is to progress; progress is teleological in nature and is able to function in this manner alone since it provides the setting for value evolvement.

Fulfillment.

Fulfillment is the resultant of a purposive entity; the property of the entity is its propositions and corresponding attributes.

Function.

Function, through its means as a process, seeks to clarify consequences of the reorganization of knowledge. To function is to act and cause.

Fusion.

Fusion is accomplished when a design is completed because all similarities have been correctly placed according to their purpose and function, and the quality of the whole has been realized through the connectives of the parts.

Future.

The future requires of the present an evaluation of the presuppositions which initiated the movement between past and present, so structuring itself that its identity can be seen, at least in part, in what now exists.

Presuppositions:
1. The future (as ends) serves as incentive in determining the construct of an organizational pattern.
2. The future is dependent for meaning upon the questions asked in the present.

G

Generalization.

The ability to generalize is dependent upon the nature of experience alone; it permits expansion of the original premises of all working hypotheses.

Presuppositions:
1. An empirical generalization, because of its nature, scope and purpose, and as existential propositions, is synthetic in probability.
2. Every generalization is hypothetical in structure; by this means it generates value conditions.
3. A generalization serves as the theoretical basis for the inductive method.
4. When a law has been validated, the generalization inherent in its premises becomes a point of origination for applicability.
5. A generalization depends upon the spontaneous functioning of the mind to provide sufficient motivation for its movement.
6. A generalization must be based on a uniformity in nature.
7. Generalization is the working hypothesis of all reflective thought.

Genius.

Genius posits the presence of something new.

Genuine.

That which is characterized as being genuine suggests that the value thus prescribed has become synonymous with its subject.

Given.

The given is but a description of one factor in an experienced problem; it is the starting point which suggests the need for analysis and study of the unknown components and posits the challenge to explanation.

Presupposition:
1. To determine a given is to relate percepts with occurrences.

Goal.

A goal is not defined by rules of method alone.

Presuppositions:

1. To determine a goal is to subject the mind to a series of metaphysical objectives which serve to open sources of potentiality.
2. Each goal is unique as it evolves from the proposition.
3. The goal is actualized when the purpose of the created subject has been realized.

Growth.

The source of growth is found in its justification; the perspective of justification is found in the value condition and value judgment.

Presupposition:

1. Mental growth is experiential growth.

Guess.

Basic to the initial step in methodology is the guess; the realization of discovery begins with the guess.

H

Harmony.

Harmony is the most single characteristic of a consciousness, intrinsically unified, whole.

Historicity.

Historicity is the being of the cosmological process.

History.

A philosophy of history is inherent in every factor of accumulation.

Holism.

Evolving from holism is a reductionism suggesting that means and end are identical.

Honesty.

The teleological factor in the scientific method is voided by means of results if intellectual honesty is not present in the analysis.

Hypothesis.

Every hypothesis is metaphysically structured and in need of analytical verification; it is a theory posited for the realization of an ideal.

Presuppositions:
1. Hypothesis is both means and end; its essence implies its role, namely, to verify the nature of the fact.
2. To actualize the meaninglessness of the material of knowledge is the prime function of the hypothesis.
3. In every hypothesis there is the intended judgment, the purpose of which is to determine the relationship between the antecedent and the effect.
4. Hypothesis learn from hypothesis as ideas learn from ideas; such learning takes place, however, only when the first hypothesis and idea has been validated and the conditions for their existence considered reliable.
5. The meaningfulness of a hypothesis is dependent upon the kinds of questions it raises.
6. Every hypothesis possesses a metaphysical base; every metaphysical base has its pragmatic components, assumptions which must be validated. It is these assumptions which require the use of metaphysical constructs for the clarification of their theories.
7. The metaphysical component in any hypothesis is logical consistency.

8. The methodology inherent in the hypothesis is based on a conditional premise. An hypothesis is the memory bank of methodology.
9. Inherent in every hypothesis is the perceptive sentence.
10. The hypothesis with the greatest number of presuppositions implies greater participation in cause.
11. The hypothesis is interested in analyzing the structure of the fact; in this way alone is the hypothesis enabled to analyze its own theories to functionally change them into suppositions.
12. To reject a hypothesis is to determine that one fact is not compatible with another fact.
13. To actualize its responsibilities, a hypothesis cannot be limited by structures placed upon it by the learner.
14. The source of the hypothesis is the implied fact; the purpose of the hypothesis is to integrate the implied fact with other facts.
15. In the structure of a hypothesis, the substance of theory is selected principles of fact.
16. To test a hypothesis is to determine whether or not its projected consequence can be actualized.
17. It is only when a hypothesis actualizes its theoretical potential that it can be declared true.
18. An hypothesis suggests the need to conceptualize the potentiality of a theory.
19. The hypothesis is developed by thought and tested by experience, the resultant of thought.
20. The value judgment underlies every working hypothesis.

I

Idea.

An idea evolves from the postulational ideas intrinsic in nature.

Presuppositions:
1. The idea is an act of the mind, in the mind, experiencing its own potential.
2. To actualize an idea is to experience its meaning; its referent is always another idea.
3. For an idea to actualize itself, the mind must enable it, by means of the process of reflective thought, to create other ideas.
4. To permit the logical faculty to exercise imagination is to develop the idea.
5. An idea is a directive making it possible for another idea to come into being.
6. It is experience which designs the idea; the logical inherent in every assumption is tested by the regulative process of verification, the methodology necessary for the analysis of any postulate or idea. An idea is the abstraction of experience.
7. An idea, as a construct, is dependent upon generalization for its initial structure.
8. An idea exists to generate other ideas.
9. The idea requires the thought process to use the potential of imagination in developing its base of operation.
10. An idea is without value unless it declares its intention.
11. The idea forces the learner to consider the implicative conditions of meaning.
12. To learn from an idea, an idea looks within, around and without.
13. The idea retains within itself the meaning of its existence

and purpose.
14. It is the idea which enables the mind to experience the material of knowledge.
15. Basic to the reasoning process and its perspective is the working hypothesis inherent in the morality of the idea.
16. As one idea is dependent on another idea for meaning, and ideas learn from ideas, the implication here suggests that the nature of an idea is dependent on its ability to determine relationships.
17. Ideas possess within themselves the need to exploit their own potential.
18. Since every idea is a product of ideas in association, no idea can be counted as being trivial.
19. The purpose of the idea is judgmental; it is to explain an existent.
20. The idea is the substantator of the real.
21. An idea, empirically based, is realized when the factual premise has been actualized.
22. An idea evolves from a setting of language, symbolic in nature.
23. To conceptualize an idea is to determine the factors which structured the idea and permitted it to evolve from a cause already unified.
24. To validate an idea is to discover its purpose.
25. To see through an idea and determine its structure is to be aware of the particulars which give to the idea its potentiality for development.
26. The idea reflects the universal in its image.
27. An idea is never a part of another idea; it functions only as a whole.

Ideal.

An ideal is established by means of a methodology based on logic.

Presuppositions:
1. Every ideal is conceived in the relationship between mind and reality.
2. The ideal is always creative.
3. In determining an ideal, the only limits imposed are those contained in potentiality.
4. An ideal carries within itself the principles underlying the justification of its existence.
5. The foundation of an ideal is need.
6. The ideal is inherent in each law of logic.
7. To create, mentally, a non-entity, is to create an ideal.
8. An ideal functions through postulational theory.
9. The ideal suggests the potentiality for creativity.
10. To estimate the value of an ideal is to determine its need.
11. To formulate an ideal is to have structured what is metaphysically possible.
12. To realize an ideal is to actualize its potential.
13. To realize an ideal is to complete the incomplete.
14. To valuate an idea is to determine an ideal.
15. An ideal is a value evolving from what is possible.

Idealism.

Idealism is the realization of value, the ground of all being.

Presuppositions:
1. Idealism has its meaning residing in experience alone; only in this way is it possible for it to develop into a dialectic.
2. To perceive meaning in existence and therefore recognize its reality is to have determined the function of idealism.
3. In idealism, the essence of reality is spiritual; its meaning lies in the perceptual world.
4. In idealism, reality is recognized by means of the antecedent factors used in its structure and organization.

5. Idealism is brought into being when an idea is recognized as real.

Identifications.

Identifications are made when the relationship between antecedents and consequences is determined.

Identify.

All principles carrying connotative value arising from the dialectical method are based upon the principle of identity; it never leads to contradictions.

Identity.

In every law of identity, the recognition which is implied reflects cause.

Imagination.

The imagination is a resultant, the reaction to the dependency of the mind upon presuppositions.

Presuppositions:
1. The essential characteristic of imagination is its ability to contemplate possibilities.
2. It is the imagination which initially destroys the concept of an entity.
3. It is impossible for the imagination to create an entity.
4. In imagination, parts become identified in wholes.
5. For imagination to be effective, it must suggest a methodology for its final realization.
6. The imagination anticipates the future.
7. To structure meaning in imagination is to have related its truth to universals.
8. As ideas feed upon ideas, the imagination must feed upon itself to gain stronger momentum.
9. Without imagination, the learner is without perspective.

Imitation.

Imitation is the cultivation of the real.

Immediacy.

The limits of immediacy can never be known.

Immediate.

The immediate is an essential component of the empirical method.

Impulse.

The directive inherent in impulse is the necessary incentive for growth.

Inclusion.

To define inclusion is to define the ability for comprehension.

Individual.

The attainment of knowledge and the experience of its meaning is the only means by which the individual is able to fulfill his potential.

Individuality.

Within function and form lies true individuality.

Induction.

The inductive process is used to provide the dimension of understanding in the learning process.

Presuppositions:
1. Induction is a demonstrable process.
2. The process of induction is dependent upon the deductive inferential before it can determine direction for its movement.
3. Induction and its processes is built into the descriptive function of deduction.
4. Induction is the movement from an idea to an idea.

5. Induction is possible only by means of perception.
6. Induction as a process is dependent upon form for its validation.
7. Because induction forms hypothesis, it is by nature selective in its process of application.
8. Inherent in the method of induction is the opportunity for self-correction.

Infer.

To infer is to act, via the idea, for the purpose of creating an awareness of potentiality. To infer logically is to establish relationships in order to determine meaning.

Inference.

Inference is the means by which the learner moves from observation to experimentation to perception on the continuum in the scientific method.

Presuppositions:

1. Without its complicative base, inference is without meaning.
2. Basic to the process of inference is the process of intellection; data serves as the foundation of thought in the process.
3. Inference evolves from quality.
4. In the process of valid inference, it is the laws in logic which describe the potentiality of a particular proposition.

Informative.

Phenomenology implies the informative; the informative unite appearance and reality.

Inquiry.

Inquiry assumes the need for a *modus operandi* to have been determined *before* the inquirer proceeds.

Presuppositions:
1. Inquiry is dependent upon the condition present in every working principle.
2. Present in every inquiry is the need to validate all laws of logic.
3. The working base of all scientific inquiry is philosophical in nature.

Insight.

Insight implies perception into a fact as well as beyond it.

Presupposition:
1. The primary dependency factor in the process of insight is its relationship with hypothesis.

Inspiration.

Inspiration makes the certification of truth possible.

Instruction.

The object of instruction is to enable the learner to educate himself.

Intangible.

Even the intangible must be tested by means of the constructs found in results.

Integration.

That which is well integrated suggests a base of a value condition which is intrinsically structured. To integrate is to use ends as means.

Intellect.

The intellect is a functionary of the mind; its only means of acting is to do so teleologically.

Presuppositions:
1. The intellect is the expression of being.

2. The intellect has two functions, the second evolving from the first: constructive and creative.
3. The task of the intellect is to interpret truth.
4. It is the intellect which permits the learner to recognize the interdependence of things.

Intellection.

The process of intellection distinguishes between the origin of knowledge and its analysis.

Presuppositions:
1. Being and its perceptual components internalize meaning making knowledge the operative force in the process of intellection.
2. Inherent within the process of intellection is a creative structure based on *a priori* presuppositions.
3. To determine the nature of values is the function of the processes of intellection.
4. The process of intellection depends upon idealism to maintain its independence.
5. The process of intellection uses the laws of logic in the dialectical confrontation between subject and object.
6. The process of intellection keeps the mind open to newly related facts.
7. The basic postulate in the process of intellection is the ability of objectivity to restructure its assumptions.
8. To predicate an ontological base for the process of intellection is to determine the implications inherent in a value condition.
9. One purpose inherent in the process of intellection is to increase self-consciousness.
10. The process of intellection defines reality by means of ideas.

Intelligence.

Intelligence is the essence of consciousness.

Presupposition:

1. The fact of intelligence assures the mind of the existence of universal.

Intent.

Intent in belief is found in the symbolization of its propositions.

Intention.

Intention is the chief motivational factor in the intellectual process.

Presuppositions:

1. Intention is implied in every concept.
2. Both intention and purpose are integral parts of a unity found in every relationship.

Intentionality.

Intentionality is the function pivot of consciousness.

Interaction.

Suggestive of the function of interaction is the potentiality of fulfillment of which the specifics of conditions possess the greatest responsibility.

Interpretation.

Interpretation, as a process, is dependent upon its conditions for its existence as well as for its validation.

Presuppositions:

1. Interpretation is always of meaning; since meaning is intentional, an interpretative quality should give evidence of intention.
2. The working principle of interpretation is organic unity.

Introspection.

Introspection is a science because of its inherent methodology.

Intuit.

To intuit is to deepen the thought processes of the mind.

Presuppositions:

1. To intuit is to perceptually objectify the material of knowledge.
2. To intuit is action of the mind as it puts itself into its object.
3. To intuit is to postulate the potentiality in a premise.
4. To intuit is to perceive relations between facts.

Intuition.

Intuition is an integral part of the thought process; it is the operative force which describes essence as being the content of existence.

Presuppositions:

1. Intuition is dependent upon analysis in determining depth in insight.
2. Intuition is an idea which has been clarified by another idea. As such it is a cognitive act arising from reflective thought.
3. Intuition determines its own essence.
4. Intuition carries the same reality factors in its essence as does any facet of empirical thought.
5. The intensity which characterizes intuition determines the depth to which the learner can experience subjective qualities.
6. Intuition precedes the act of judgment in the process of intellection.
7. The object of intuition is determined while in the act of determining its own essence.
8. To act intuitively is to have found meaning in the object of learning.

9. The most potent force underlying the process of intellection making intuition possible is the value condition.

Investigation.

An integral part of every epistemological investigation is the metaphysical question.

Is.

What *is* possesses generic strength, and becomes so because of its meaning.

J

Judge.

To judge on the basis of a value assertion is to negate another judgment; it is to methodically determine a basis for comparison, proceeding from the working base of the hypothesis of fact.

Judgment.

Truth consists of many strands of implicative values; to determine the validity of each inherent relationship of the compossible is to judge. Judgment is an act of reconstructing a setting; it is valuational in nature when its referents evolve from value conditions.

Presuppositions:
1. The value condition presupposes the value judgment; the determination of reality presupposes the act of judgment.
2. Conditions are presupposed in every judgment which determine the degree of awareness inherent in implicative value.
3. Because of the fallibility of sense data, every empirical judgment, since it is largely based on sense data, is fallible.
4. To make an error in judgment is to fail to recognize the

implications of its inferences.
5. An ethical judgment is either true or false.
6. Judgment is always in the light of experience.
7. From the value condition judgment arises; from the process of deduction inference arises; both of these concepts are confronted by the responsibility of logic before they become an integral part of reflective thought.
8. Every judgment implies a system of postulates.
9. Every judgment has value references.
10. The value judgment is the verification of an existent.
11. The value judgment concerns absolutes when its premises have been validated.
12. To make a value judgment is to have justified the basic premise contained in every condition.
13. To define a value judgment is to objectify its implications.
14. In every value judgment lies an ontological premise; it is this premise which permits the judgment to be based on a proposition which has as its function to evaluate.
15. The value judgment is validated when the relationship between the ideal and reality has been determined.

Justification.

To justify is to trace the history of causal relations.

Presupposition:

1. Self-justification is the process of conditioning, an intellection of the existent and the possible.

K

Know.

To develop a perspective is to apprehend another level of truth; to know is to possess truth by objectifying its relative values.

Knowability.

The condition of knowability evolves from the relationship inherent in form and matter and their dependency upon cause.

Knowing.

Knowing is the realization that the content of the material of knowledge has been structured by the mind.

Presuppositions:

1. To determine the characteristics inherent in the oppositional stance between the known and the knowing process is to structure the latter on an objectified methodological base.
2. The occurrence of knowing and validating its objects is the function of the epistemological thrust.
3. The process of knowing is dependent upon the content and structure of the material of knowledge.
4. The responsibility of knowing is to identify the relationship between the material of knowledge and its structure.
5. The science of knowing is characterized by the principles inherent in the relationships existing among problems.

Knowledge.

Knowledge cannot be separated from its material or content; it is actualized by the mind only when the instrumentation of content is realized for its potentiality.

Presuppositions:

1. The acquisition of knowledge is a process requiring developmental intention as the source of its movement.
2. Adequacy of knowledge is realized when the relation between an idea and its object has been determined.
3. Knowledge makes the distinction between appearance and reality.
4. *A priori* knowledge is the realization of the meaningfulness

of relationships.
5. The underlying assumptions of knowledge and its material imply a universality of application.
6. Knowledge is attained when its material is abstracted to the point of tautology. The degree of knowledge attained is dependent on the quality of the relationships determinated between ideas.
7. Knowledge is attained by direct awareness alone.
8. The conceptual element of knowledge is its interpretative responsibility.
9. A conceptual unit of knowledge arises from the degree of perception implying the level of depth in understanding.
10. The content of the material of knowledge is what has happened.
11. Degrees of knowledge are attained when the dependency factor between facts are realized and actualized by the mind; that is, when principles at work uniting two facts proffer an explanation and suggest meaning.
12. Since knowledge is always intentional, it is also direct.
13. Knowledge is discovery.
14. Knowledge by description is dependent upon the process underlying the concept of inference.
15. Even though the knowledge of essence is transitive, the knowledge of the dimensions of its existence is intransitive.
16. All knowledge evolves from existents; this does not imply, however, that knowledge and its material are external to the mind.
17. All knowledge is experiential.
18. All knowledge gained directs a light beyond itself.
19. All knowledge and its material is dependent upon inference.
20. All knowledge is introspective in nature.
21. Knowledge cannot exist apart from logic.
22. The material of knowledge, for its acquisition, requires a

mastery of the principle of reason, as well as the use of the process of conceptualization.
23. Inherent within the material of knowledge is a testable process for the validation of its own constructs.
24. The material of knowledge as content is an integrated whole; within the whole lies the methodology necessary for the realization of its parts.
25. The material of knowledge is determinate in all of its relationships; it is this factor which makes it possible for the mind to understand.
26. All knowledge is being; to make its material intelligible is to objectify its form and function.
27. The implications of the material of knowledge express an ethical relationship inherent within the structure of its being.
28. All material of knowledge is inferential.
29. The material of knowledge is the controlling factor in the process of intellection.
30. The material of knowledge implies both method and content, each dependent upon the other for meaning.
31. The material of knowledge, in order to be known, is dependent upon the rational abilities of the mind.
32. The material of knowledge is actualized by the mind and motivated by the power inherent in the potentiality of its content.
33. The material of knowledge serves as its own premises.
34. The material of knowledge is not the subject of predicates; the subject of predicates is the correlatives found in meaning.
35. The material of knowledge is structured by means of form and function both of which are determined by order.
36. To know the material of knowledge is to experience its being.
37. Mediate knowledge is conceptual knowledge.

38. The nature of knowledge evolves from a dialectical base of noncontradiction. This means that the learning process involves all facets of the material of knowledge synthetically structured by means of organismically controlled connectives.
39. New knowledge is re-constructed knowledge, the mind building upon progress rather than change; the process is one of self-correction.
40. To be aware of the implicative values inherent in the material of knowledge is to be conscious of the object of knowledge.
41. Knowledge is an organism the parts of which are interdependent.
42. The implications inherent in the possession of knowledge insist upon the presence of other reality factors (such as other minds) in the process of intellection.
43. From the material of knowledge arises the postulates which make it possible to experience their meaning.
44. Potentiality in the material of knowledge is determined first in its source, namely, being; it is the being of thought.
45. The basic presupposition underlying all knowledge is a cognizant subject.
46. The presupposition of knowledge is the working hypothesis.
47. All knowledge is problematic.
48. The primary responsibility of knowledge is to insist that the whole is seen in relation to its parts.
49. The resultant of knowledge is action-, projected or already realized; implied in action is the actualization of its material by the mind.
50. Scientific knowledge is a construct of the existent; it explains what has become real to the learner.
51. Self knowledge presupposes the existence of a self-realized learner whose capacity for critical judgment is inherent in

his powers of consciousness.
52. Basic to any problem and its analysis is its material; it is this material or content which is the source of knowledge.
53. The source of knowledge is perceived fact.
54. Every theory of knowledge is self-justifying.
55. To achieve knowledge is to possess a knowledge of the material of reality and synthesize its material.
56. To acquire knowledge is to be conscious of the essence of its material.
57. To experience knowledge is to find meaning in its material.
58. To possess knowledge is to be aware of the meaningfulness of its material; the possession of knowledge is the determiner of existence.
59. To possess knowledge is to realize the synthetic quality of the ontological base of its material.
60. To use knowledge is to use its potentiality.
61. The virtue of knowledge lies in its potentiality.

Known.

The known, as being, is always in the process of becoming meaningful.

Presuppositions:
1. The known must be explained in terms of the known.
2. Existence and essence are synonymous terms in the same way we say to be known is to be.

L

Language.

Language is the expression of thought; thought is expressive of awareness.

Presuppositions:

1. The cognitive function of language incorporates within its aims the metaphysical delineation of categories.
2. Language is controlled by its definitions.
3. Language is the most powerful form of energy available to the learner.
4. Language unites ideas and form.
5. Language is the prime factor in determining meaning in experience.
6. The utilitarian qualities of language are recognized in their creative potential.
7. It is the structural potentiality inherent in language which determines the depth of thought.

Law.

Law is a resultant in the determination of the implicative value evolving from every causal relationship.

Presuppositions:

1. The function of law arises from its natural methodologically oriented principle of explanation.
2. Natural law is subject to but one change: that which takes place in the mind.
3. The specificity of cause is found in its ability to generate generalizations equating these with natural law.

Laws.

Laws validate theory in its relation to perceptual objects.

Presuppositions:

1. Laws are determined by the determinants inherent in end-means relationship.
2. Phenomena is built upon laws which must be discovered by the mind; laws in contradiction one to another suggest that

the causative factors under consideration have not as yet been determined.
3. Laws evolve from intention.
4. Laws can be known; as a result, laws are *a priori* to facts.
5. All laws, by nature, are empirically based, and refer to universals first, and only secondly to particulars.
6. Causal laws imply necessity.
7. Ontological laws can be discovered only by means of the process of abstraction.
8. Laws exist to make it possible for premises to be established and validated.
9. As laws develop they make it possible for premises to reduce their conditions.
10. Laws are based upon the principles underlying each fact.
11. A postulate is presupposed in every scientific law.
12. Scientific laws and universality evolve from the same cause.

Learn.

To learn is to condition the mind to teleologically define the part of the material of knowledge.

Learner.

The learner is interpenetrated with a sense of the educative aspects of process.

Presuppositions:
1. The task of the creative learner is to discover the ideal and express the potential of being.
2. The creative learner learns to make further learning possible.
3. In self-education, the learner enables the idea to grow.
4. For the learner to transcend himself, it implies movement from the physical to the spiritual place of existence
5. The purpose of the learner is to determine the conditions

under which knowledge is attained.
6. The first responsibility of the learner is to transcend all facts of his learning which remain relative in his mind.
7. The task of the learner is to inquire into the conditions which make knowledge and its material discoverable.
8. The learner is a synthesis of ideas; his task is to create values.
9. The true learner is a believer in the power of the human will.
10. The learner creates himself as a process in order to learn. Thus, his primary concern is with the question of morality.
11. The true learner works toward greater consciousness.

Learning.

To have learned is to imply that communication has taken place.

Presuppositions:

1. Inherent within the material of knowledge is its conative value; to experience such value is to learn.
2. Learning reveals the concept of learning as presuppositions.
3. All learning is a creative act; it is the process of logical deduction, the reduction of opposites inherent in every part, of identifying a part with a whole.
4. All learning begins with experience.
5. All learning possesses a certain intensity.
6. Learning is the language of idealism.
7. To learn is to visualize the object of learning.
8. To learn is to absorb the principles underlying the relationships among facts.
9. The process of learning, in each step of its movement, reveals new forms as well as new intellectual forces.
10. The learning process is concerned with depth in apprehension and comprehension; without this, learning as a process ceases.
11. The function of the process of learning is to bring existents

into being.
12. The process of learning receives its incentive as well as direction from the powers of reason.
13. All learning is purposive in nature; this is what determines its pragmatic character.
14. To experience is to learn; true learning is to experience what is found meaningful in the material of knowledge.

Limitations.

Limitations imposed through methodology make for clarity and transparency.

Presupposition:
1. Limitations are integral parts of every supposition underlying order. Within the structure of order is movement, the type of which makes limitations viable.

Logic.

Logic teaches the learner *how* to know.

Presuppositions:
1. Abstraction is a basic ingredient of logic.
2. Logic is synonymous with being.
3. Logic is the operative revelatory force evolving from cause.
4. Without creative thought, logic is without direction and its law cannot be validated.
5. To function as law, logic is dependent upon the validated evidence which serves as the construct in its presuppositions.
6. Logic engenders the hypothesis in order to assure itself the freedom necessary for analysis.
7. Because the character of logic can best be described as instrumental, it is in this capacity it best serves as the organizer of knowledge.

8. All logic is intentional in nature; in this way it serves as the source of instrumentation in every methodological pattern.
9. Logic is subject to laws; laws are based upon principles evolving from cause.
10. Unless the laws of logic are applicable, they are meaningless.
11. Each law of logic is dependent upon propositional concepts to validate cause.
12. Laws of logic, in order to function adequately, eliminate all paradoxes and contradictions in the nature of its object.
13. Whatever limitations are found in the laws of logic are imposed by the science of metaphysics in its design of concepts.
14. Each law of logic has its point of origination in metaphysics.
15. All criteria for validating the laws of logic are problematic in nature.
16. Logic enables the learner to interpret the material of knowledge.
17. Since all methodology is based on logical principles, logic depends upon its own principles to validate its own methodology.
18. It is logic which permits the mind to act as a discoverer.
19. Logic is intrinsically motivated by a recognition of its own needs.
20. All logic is inductive in nature.
21. The functional premises of logic serve as the metaphysical bases of ontology.
22. As laws, logic is operational; their concern is primarily with the learning process.
23. Presupposed in every law of logic is the transcendental quality of conceptualization and its implicative values.
24. Principles of logic are determined in the confrontation

between mind, fact and methodology.
25. To determine the function of a variable and ascertain its relation to other parts, and the parts to the whole, is the responsibility of logic.
26. To determine need and analyze its nature is the first responsibility of logic.
27. To design, formulate and determine structure, as the primary responsibility of logic, is to identify universals in particulars, and particulars in universals.
28. Logic is the tool for the exposition and clarification of ideas.

M

Man.

Man is the subject-matter of education, and the source of value.

Presuppositions:

1. Man, as the embodiment of existence, synthesizes the finite and the infinite for the actualization of his being.
2. It is only as man recognizes and accepts the fact that universals exist in him, that he exists in that which is universal.

Matter.

All matter (material of knowledge) is based on value conditions.

Presuppositions:

1. While matter is finite, and therefore imperfect, the infinite attributes of matter are functional and evolve from mind as applicable cause and are therefore absolute.
2. Matter realizes itself in being.
3. Matter, as potentiality, is in a constant state of change.
4. Within matter are the resources necessary for the structure

of form and function.
5. It is the forms of matter which are reproduced and not matter itself.
6. Matter, as finite, functions only as potentiality.
7. All matter implies potentiality.
8. To intuit the potentiality of matter is to conceptualize its powers of application.
9. Form and function serve to characterize the potentiality of being in matter.
10. The scope of matter lies in its teleological nature.
11. Matter becomes known only as substance or content, the material of knowledge.

Meaning.

To find meaning is to be conscious of the synthetic qualities of the material of knowledge and recognize the potentiality inherent in each connective in the relationship between parts.

Presuppositions:
1. Meaning is found only in relation to an absolute.
2. Meaning is an absolute but subject to change in the mind. As an interpretation subject to change, it is the factor of substitution which permits the replacement of one absolute for another.
3. All meaning is intentional, and, as such, is an intended act.
4. To function as a universal, meaning implies the need for the mind to reflect, and through reflection, unify parts with wholes and wholes with wholes.
5. Inherent within meaning is the potentiality for the development of categories.
6. Meaning clarifies the unclear and structures the nebulous.
7. The chief characteristic of meaning is coherence.
8. Conceptual meaning is universal.
9. Meaning must be confirmed by definition as well as by

inferential values.
10. Meaning is the cue of all knowledge; it is the ultimate frame of reference to determine whether or not learning has taken place.
11. To find meaning in data requires the same process as to find form in matter.
12. When meaning has been determined, the distinction between the knowing subject and the object known has been removed.
13. To express meaning is to have determined purpose inherent in the object of meaning.
14. Meaning unites fact with value.
15. Full meaning is realized when a totality of comprehension suggest unity of thought.
16. Inherent within meaning are teleological implications; the function of meaning is to give birth to new ideas.
17. The genesis of meaning lies in the conditions which foster the need for the value judgment.
18. To have found meaning is to understand the idea through the process of conceptualization in the complicative values of data.
19. To become aware of the implicative values in meaning is to have deductively set in motion the process of intellection.
20. Meaning, to retain its logicality, depends upon a referent.
21. Meaning is present only with lucidity.
22. As one fact is included in another fact, meaning is included in meaning by means of the implicative values in both.
23. Meaning is the means of knowing.
24. It is the mind which functions, not apprehended meaning; cognitively, meaning is the resultant of a metaphysically oriented determinant.
25. Inherent within the perspective of meaning is the structured nature of fact.

26. Meaning is the object or material known.
27. The ontological premise of meaning is the word *is*.
28. The operational theory of meaning must include the relational factor which permits two ideas to unite for the purpose of conceptualization.
29. Meaning and its projected perspectives evolve from reflective thought.
30. Meaning fulfills the potentiality of an existent.
31. Meaning designs patterns of analysis and methodologies conducive to the determination of complicative values in all referents.
32. Meaning is achieved only within the context of reflective thought.
33. Meaning is identical with thought and projects the ideal in experience.
34. To derive meaning is to associate one fact with another.
35. To experience meaning is to actualize the nature of certainty.
36. To experience meaning is to have realized an existent.
37. To experience meaning is to have ontologically interpreted its systems.
38. To find meaning is to have experienced a reality already tested for reliability and validity.
39. To qualify meaning requires the resources of an existentially oriented mind.
40. To structure meaning is to rely upon connotative implications.
41. Totality of meaning is fully realized only when all facts in a system are united and form a whole.
42. Meaning implies the attainment of a level of truth; its intention is to determine direction.
43. The implicative values inherent in meaning connote intention of application.

Meaningfulness.

Meaningfulness is achieved when the implications in a hypothesis are realized, and the comparison is made between implications and fact.

Meanings.

Meanings are parts of an objectively ordered whole.

Presupposition:

1. All meanings are intentional in nature, responding to the reflective process, the creation of intellect.

Means.

Means are functionaries of the value condition.

Presuppositions:

1. The construct of means is the same for ends.
2. Ends demand the same quality of control as do means.
3. It is means which forbids ends to impose themselves on the learner.
4. Means must be evident in the completed construct of an idea.
5. An integral part of means is its teleological perspective.
6. To structure means is to objectify the teleological process; this is done by means of the hypothesis when the hypothesis is used as something more than a technique.

Mechanization.

Mechanization destroys the potentiality of freedom.

Memory.

Memory is the ability to create from the known new conditions out of which new facts may arise.

Metaphysics.

Metaphysics is a methodological perspective which has as its aim revelation of the whole by means of determining the reality of its parts.

Presuppositions:
1. Metaphysics, by means of its presuppositions, is the most critical apparatus in the science of analysis.
2. All dimensions of the science of metaphysics are hypothetical in nature.
3. Perception provides metaphysics with its enabling power; this arises through insight into the means-end relationship.
4. All dimensions of metaphysics are based on epistemology.
5. Metaphysics, by means of method, defines existence in terms of its truth.
6. Metaphysics places all objects of knowledge is an experiential context.
7. Metaphysics calls for an understanding of the relationship between form and content.
8. The science of metaphysics functions so as to destroy all distinctions between the theoretical and the practical.
9. The function of metaphysics is to synthesize the material of knowledge.
10. The functional responsibilities of metaphysics are determined by means of the analytical method.
11. Metaphysics is the means whereby inquiry validates its factual bases.
12. Metaphysics possess no logical limitations.
13. The working base of metaphysics is logic.
14. Metaphysics, as the quest for truth, seeks first for the clarification of meaning.
15. The method of metaphysics is reflective thought.
16. Metaphysics is without perspective if its methodology ignores observation, experimentation and perception.
17. Metaphysics is the methodology of process; in this capacity it provides the setting in which fact can evolve from principle and become identified with a unified structure.

18. Metaphysics is inferential in nature.
19. Metaphysics permits the learner to become conscious of all potentialities in experience.
20. Metaphysics possesses but one presupposition, that is, the nature, scope and purpose of epistemology.
21. Metaphysics brings to a proposition an historical setting, a presupposition projecting the meaningfulness of absolutes.
22. In metaphysics, absolute presuppositions serve as hypotheses.
23. The objectifier of being is the science of metaphysics; metaphysics functions by means of its methodological principles.
24. Metaphysics is the art of reflective thought structured by the scientific method.
25. The responsibility of metaphysics is to be fully aware of the implicative values in every fact. Principles and causes are the primary responsibility of metaphysics.
26. Inherent within the structures of metaphysics is an objectivity designed to function using as its base of operation the scientific method.
27. The subject matter of metaphysics is being and its correlates.
28. Metaphysics unites knowledge and reality.
29. It is metaphysics which determines the relationship between value and understanding.

Method.

Method is reflective of the ability for abstraction.

Presuppositions:

1. The aim of method is objectivity.
2. Method functions by means of categories.
3. Method has as one of its responsibilities the clarification of context.

4. Intelligibility, transparency and inclusiveness are the regulatory factors controlling method.
5. When theory is applied through law, and universals are revealed through particulars, the deductive method has been used.
6. The deductive method is dependent upon an ability to conceptualize meaning in every relationship before it can develop a construct in the analysis of an idea.
7. The deductive method requires the use of assumptions, out of which propositions arise for the purpose of delineating generalizations.
8. The deductive method, the process of which is based on meaning, recognizes its dependency upon the empirical procedure formulated by the inductive method.
9. To move from presuppositions to premises to conclusions is the essence of the deductive method.
10. When the deductive method is functioning, it is explaining. To explain, it is dependent upon the process of reason.
11. Consistency and continuity are two of the most important goals of the deductive method.
12. Experience alone makes it possible for the learner to handle the metaphysical components of the deductive method and control the factors of prejudgment in the realization of meaning.
13. Propositions evolve from propositions as ideas evolve from ideas, the method employed in both instances is the deductive.
14. The scope of the deductive method involves a synthesis of its teleological components.
15. The primary characteristic of the deductive method is transcendence.
16. To use the deductive method is to determine the validity of specific premises in the formulation of working hypotheses.

17. Epistemologically, the dialectical method is concerned with the totality of knowledge.
18. In determining the degree of learning, the method of the dialectic in the learning process implies a need to reveal contradictions in the process itself.
19. Only an empirical method is able to discern the concepts inherent in change.
20. Method is the means chosen to clarify empirical procedures.
21. Method is the structuring of experiential values.
22. To extend the implications of method is to bridge the physical and metaphysical realms of existence.
23. The primary responsibility of the inductive method is the development of hypotheses.
24. The operational factor inherent in the inductive method is the ontological perspective of each relational principle realized from among facts.
25. The inductive method is the process most conducive to the learner's need for determining potentiality.
26. The inductive method infers prediction.
27. The inductive method demands the need to discover the principles underlying the relationship between facts.
28. The purpose of investigative method is to discover truth.
29. Method is the means of implementation chosen by the mind in the act of functioning.
30. An integral part of method is the power of perception.
31. Method is always prescriptive.
32. There is a prescriptive sense in which method reveals its scope.
33. The purpose of method is to enable the learner to know; the process of knowing is a continuous one implying the need to delimit the learning milieu.
34. Method is not an ultimate.
35. The scientific method is the means of implementation to

relate one fact to another and determine the working principles of each.
36. The scientific method cannot analyze a phenomena in isolation.
37. While the scientific method is a process of analysis, within the process are graduations of comprehension each of which are structured by value conditions and judgments.
38. Discovery is the functional goal of the scientific method.
39. The scientific method is the investigative procedure devised to analyze objects as wholes.
40. The scientific method has the task of reproducing the object in the subject.
41. To test method is to determine the validity of means and ends.

Methodology.

The structure of any methodology, to be logical, must be dependent upon the perspective of a scientific law.

Presuppositions:

1. All methodology *intends* definition.
2. Methodology is the instrument of discovery.
3. The empirical base of all inductive methodology is the ontological premise of mathematics, thus permitting methodology to serve as a means of instrumentation.
4. Since the power of metaphysics lies in its ability for transcendence, it is the methodology which brings this insight into being which the scientific perspective incorporates within itself.
5. Methodology implies order; to determine order, the material of knowledge relating to the particular responsibility of method in a particular instance must be known.
6. All methodology is pragmatic.
7. All methodology can be characterized as possessing a

reflexive temper; this temper arises from the theoretical base of analysis.
8. A methodology is bibliographic in scope.
9. Inherent in every methodology is the transcendent factor which controls the structure of definition.

Mind.

The mind is the idea in action.

Presuppositions:
1. The mind discovers its ability for abstraction and synthesization by means of the analysis of the synthetic qualities of the material of knowledge.
2. The mind is able to integrate and unify only after it has first determined the factors which make each fact a distinct working principle yet dependent for existence on other facts.
3. The mind and its activity cannot be separated.
4. It is impossible for the mind to transcend the act of perception.
5. It is the mind which actualizes the fact and its dependency relationships; mind theorizes potentiality by means of the material of knowledge.
6. The mind, as an universal, is a structure designed by its relationship to objective reality.
7. Mind is being itself in search for the being of consciousness.
8. The categorical implicator of the mind is the interpretative function of metaphysics.
9. The process of intellection requires the mind to recognize that all cause resides in the being of the material of knowledge.
10. The mind functions through concepts.
11. The conceptual base from which the mind functions permits it to use the inductive method in its search for knowledge.
12. The mind is always concerned with ultimate questions.

13. Mind is both constitutive and instrumental.
14. The creative mind must have specifics in the material of knowledge with which to work.
15. The creative mind is highly selective in its choice of materials through which it works.
16. As the mind categorizes its essence, it is depending upon the metaphysical implications of its process of intellection.
17. At any stage of development, the mind functions as a process evolving from the totality of experience.
18. Through experience the mind formulates new presuppositions which enables it to further experience meaning.
19. The mind functions only as it apprehends meaning; that is, when two or more ideas meet in dialogue.
20. The mind functions as the self experiences meaning.
21. There is a determinate factor in all self-consciousness; it is this determinate which permits experience to integrate mind and reality.
22. The mind finds meaning only in that which is teleological nature.
23. Only through the mind is anything meaningful.
24. As the mind functions, it becomes increasingly aware of the ontological principles underlying its own methodology.
25. Both existence and essence assume a type of relationship with objects which make it mandatory for the mind to identify itself with the object of learning which serves as the premise of belief.
26. It is the idea which keeps projecting its own presuppositions that must be watched carefully as the learner attempts to help his mind open to all ideas.
27. It is only the perceptually based mind which will be able to distinguish between general and particular facts.
28. Mind uses the potentiality of meaning to actuate its process

of intellection.
29. Inherent within the process of perception is the operative factor of the ability of the mind for transcendence. This factor is dependent upon the value judgment for its momentum.
30. Mind functions as the process of perception in its relationship to the object.
31. The mind functions by means of its propositions.
32. When the mind reflects upon itself, it acts logically.
33. The mind functions only in relation to the relational factors inherent in universals and their particulars.
34. The task of the mind is to determine the relevancy of the real by means of its many structures.
35. Mind, at any given moment, bespeaks a totality of being; while it can transcend itself, it functions as mind in the process.
36. The greatest task of the mind is to validate its own actions.

Mistakes.

Mistakes are inevitable if assumptions are based on evidence not yet validated.

Mode.

Mode must be identified with the potential of being.

Motion.

Motion, as an event, is cause.

N

Nature.

Inherent in nature, as cause, is the structure and perspective of reason.

Presuppositions:

1. The character of nature expresses itself via the reality of the universe.
2. The intelligence of nature bespeaks the ideal in cause.
3. The operational factor in nature is causal law.
4. Form, function, and the potentiality for design in form, is intrinsic to nature.
5. The purpose of nature is to actualize itself in the human mind.
6. Nature is synonymous with value.

Necessary.

Whatever is necessary has no alternative.

Necessity.

Historical necessity is the foundation of belief.

Presuppositions:

1. Every true proposition is dependent upon logical necessity for validation.
2. Relationships evolving from necessity provide the requirements for any projection via implications.

Newness.

Creation implies evaluation; evaluation implies newness; newness is a resultant of consciousness.

Norm.

A norm is a human ideal; it is derived deductively.

Presuppositions:

1. The norm serves as the working hypothesis for the development of a concept; in this way it provides direction for the learning process.

2. Learning takes place only when the learner has determined the source of validity in the hypothesis which serves as the norm for the discovery of purpose in every fact.

O

Object.

An object *is* and *becomes* what its potential possesses; it possesses both past and a future.

Presuppositions:
1. Every object reveals opportunities for abstraction.
2. The nature of an object expresses the history of the development of that object by means of its *reason* for existence.
3. Every object contains the potentiality for wholeness.
4. No object can be separate from its subject. Experience does not permit it. The subject of every object is the goal subsumed in its potential.
5. To cognize an object is to experience its subject.
6. To identify an object is to identify both its existence and essence.
7. To know an object implies that the object must exist prior to its being known.
8. To qualify an object is to determine the nature of the qualities of that object and the value conditions which first brought it into being.
9. To use an object is to have perceived the nature of the value conditions which first brought it into being.
10. Inherent in the object is its value.

Objective.

To test an objective is to determine the distinctive qualities of certainty and truth.

Objectivity.

Objectivity implies the presence of direction; to maintain this perspective, it is dependent upon the direction of the value condition.

Presuppositions:

1. The process of determining objectivity relies on a methodology which has developed a means of isolating those factors which have brought a particular object into being.
2. There is a subjective element in all objectivity since no existent is independent of, or extrinsic to, consciousness.
3. To define objectivity is the only means of using its implications in value judgment.

Observation.

Observation presupposes the actualization of experience; it is acting on assumptions. Mere observation reveals facts alone.

Presuppositions:

1. To observe is to draw a conclusion from recognized presuppositions; it is to experience the means for the achievement of the potential.
2. Observation is a record of what is seen; perception is the inscription of all experience.
3. One of the functions of observation is to design new hypotheses.
4. Observation gives rise to generalizations about an existent.
5. The key to observation is knowing what to observe and why.
6. Perceptual observation is dependent upon depth in interpretation to validate its conclusions.
7. To observe perceptually is to become conscious of the cues

present in every hypothesis.
8. To observe perceptually is to determine the principles and characteristics which unite two or more facts. This is possible only in the open and inquiring mind.
9. To observe is to determine the potential in a perspective.
10. True observation requires a mind methodologically oriented and perceptually based.
11. To observe is the first step in the process of verification; when the act of observation has involved the methodology of perception, the first step in the process of interpretation has been taken.
12. The vision gained through observation is the means by which the mind transcends the limits inherent in every existent.

Observer.

The observer has the responsibility of relating what he perceives to what he knows.

Presupposition:

1. The true observer is aware of the meaningfulness of totalities.

Occurrence.

Every occurrence is change.

Oneself.

To know oneself is to know those things which comprise the self.

Ontology.

Contrary to the epistemological responsibility of ontology is the belief that entities exist.

Presuppositions:

1. Ontology bespeaks an interest in ultimates and the absolute;

to perceive from an ontological base is to determine the nature of existents as well as their potential.
2. Without purpose, ontology is meaningless. The function of ontology, therefore, is to provide the processional intent in learning.
3. The language of ontology implies a theoretical premise.
4. The science of ontology permits the perceiver to be aware of differences and potentiality.

Order.

That which exists is reciprocally impossible; order arises from correlativity alone.

Presuppositions:

1. Principles of order determine the construct of every law of logic.
2. The qualities found in order are determined by the logical constructs of its structure.
3. Implied in order as a structure, based on laws of logic, is cause determined by mind.
4. To actualize order is to actualize the teleological nature of process.

Organism.

An organism is a hypothetical environment in which thought seeks to function.

Presuppositions:

1. An organism, functioning as its own creative environment, becomes an integral part of the process of intellection when it asserts its adaptive abilities.
2. Inherent within an organism are self-sustaining qualities, all of which permit the organism to function teleologically in order to maintain its perspective.

Origins.

Origins are found only in existents.

P

Particular.

It is the particular which makes the universal a reality and meaningful.

Presuppositions:
1. Particulars make it possible for the act of cognition to function.
2. To be aware of particulars, their nature and potentiality, is to intuit the meaningfulness of the material of knowledge.
3. Particulars are existents rather than descriptors of existence.
4. Like deduction, induction transcends particulars.
5. Like a universal, a particular has meaning only in relation to what has already been validated by the mind.
6. To comprehend the meaning of a particular and determine the nature of its essence is to discover the factors which determine its individuality.
7. Universals comprise particular objects; particulars are universalized by the mind through the process of experience.
8. When seen in relation to universals, particulars exert their potentiality by means of their representational nature.
9. Each universal comprises a world of particulars none of which are entities; to determine value in the object of a particular is to predicate object as subject and equate it with consciousness.

Parts.

Characteristic of every part is its affinity to a whole.

Presuppositions:

1. To understand the part is to perceive it in its relation to the whole.
2. In each part there is a content or material which can be found in every other part of the whole.

Pattern.

To perceive a contextual pattern is to infer a conclusion from categorical premises.

Perceive.

To perceive is to analyze the real.

Presuppositions:

1. To perceive is to correct, if necessary, its own assumptions.
2. To perceive is to experience the meaningfulness of structure; it is to experience meaning.
3. To perceive is to have been intrinsically motivated by the perspective of cause.
4. To perceive is to experience the structure of that which is potential.
5. To perceive is to think reflectively.
6. To perceive is to analyze structure.

Perception.

The process of perceiving inevitably involves a dependency on relationships such as the distinction between *about* and *of* in the material of knowledge.

Presuppositions:

1. It is the assumptions found in the process of perception

which make it impossible for entities to exist.
2. The mind which functions from a perceptual base dissolves the subjective ingredients of chance.
3. Perception is a cognitive function.
4. Perception functions as consciousness when based on the principles of idealism.
5. Perception is dependent upon understanding for realization in its process of deduction.
6. The function of perception is to reveal the nature of the real.
7. Perception is the base from which inference operates; impressions gained by means of perception give birth to new ideas.
8. There is no perception without an accompanying interpretation.
9. The learner is unable to perceive until the senses are recognized only for their presuppositional perspectives.
10. Perception implies the ability for application; to perceive is to experience the applicative agents inherent in the material of knowledge.
11. The mind of perception functions by means of the ideas it projects.
12. Perception has only one object, the actualization of reality by the mind. In perception, the object being perceived must become the subject of reflection.
13. The penetrative quality of the perception determines the quality of the awareness necessary to fully realize the potentiality of the object perceived.
14. Perception relates to parts as well as to wholes.
15. The resultant of any perception is more than the limitations of a delineation.
16. The process of perception is selective; it is an awareness that the observer is an integral part of that which he observes.

17. The qualities of sensual perception are limited to the interpretative abilities of mental perception.
18. For the mind, an event is the act of perception; perception is the structure found in every inter-relationship, the working base of all intra-dependencies.
19. To perceive implies a perceiver; while the subject matter of perception resides outside of the perceiver, the act of perception incorporates the subject matter and makes it an integral part of the mind.
20. Perception is a process of expressing the symbolic.
21. A basic operative force in the theory of knowledge is the process of perception.
22. Perception and thought are inter-dependent concepts based on the perspective of resemblance; resemblance requires the use of the selective process of evaluation.
23. As the most complex and sophisticated ingredient in the process of intellection perception alone brings about understanding.

Percepts.

Percepts are an integral part of every transcendental process.

Permanence.

The main characteristic of permanence is its relativity because of the conditions which assures it its existence. Existence bespeaks totality.

Person.

Creativity begins with and revolves about the self. This implies the need for the creative person to fully use the self.

Perspective.

The learner's perspective conies to him from the metaphysical implicatives in every potential.

Phenomenon.

Every phenomenon, suggestive of reality rather than appearance, combining fact with fact, is purposive in scope.

Philosophize.

To philosophize means to synthesize one's own thought processes. It is to determine the conditions conducive to thinking in depth.

Presuppositions:

1. To philosophize is to analyze meaning.
2. To philosophize is to experience meaning on all levels of existence.

Philosophy.

Philosophy is the embodiment of the ability of the mind to intuitively subject all existence to the process of actualization and its need to determine potentiality.

Presuppositions:

1. Philosophy has as its point of origination the synthesis of facts and their principles.
2. The purpose of philosophy is to generate reflective thought.
3. Philosophy is the science of unifying and integrating meaning in human thought.

Polarity.

Polarity implies the presence of an internal structure presupposing permanency within relativity and a consistency within process.

Position.

To verify a metaphysical position is to do so in principle alone.

Possibility.

To determine a possibility is to uncover a need.

Postulate.

A postulate is a condition underlying methodological principles for the discovery of truth; its purpose is cognitive in function, providing a critical apparatus for the realization of existence.

Presuppositions:

1. The purpose of a postulate is to prepare the groundwork and setting in which the proposition can function as a reducible element arising from each logical relationship.
2. A postulate is transparent; implicit in the postulate are the implicative values making it possible for the deductive method to function.
3. Postulates and techniques have as their goal the substantiation of the material of knowledge.

Potentiality.

Potentiality resides in determinants; determinants possess the directives for change found in every alternative. It is this factor which leads the learner to postulate a new hypothesis.

Presuppositions:

1. Potentiality is the most important condition of an act.
2. Potentiality is the reason underlying belief and its activity.
3. Potentiality is reducing change to intelligibility.
4. Potentiality is determined only after its factual base has been experienced.
5. The functional base of potentiality is its structured perspective.
6. To realize potentiality is to actualize existence in the existential mind; this is done by means of the manipulation of conditions.
7. Potentiality resides in the validation of fact.

Power.

As an operational factor, power is dependent upon relationships inherent in change for the realization of its potentiality.

Presupposition:
1. A creative, critical power is necessary for the learner to possess if he is to develop his ability for conceptualization.

Prediction.

Prediction involves the use of the differential qualities found in the inductive method; its perspective pertains only to matters of fact.

Presuppositions:
1. Prediction is based on the degree of apprehension in cause.
2. Prediction is one responsibility of the inductive method.

Premise.

A premise may be based upon presuppositions or on laws of logic. From these evolve assumptions, theoretically based, but having as their function the discovery of principles.

Presuppositions:
1. If a premise has been validated and declared true, the conclusion can be declared true as well. An integral part of every premise is the potentiality to declare a conclusion.
2. All epistemological premises are revealed in categories; since a category is ontological in nature, such a premise depends upon the logic of universals.
3. From a factual premise evolves an evaluative conclusion.
4. To perceive the nature of an ontological premise is to see universals in particulars.
5. A premise as well as its validity (methods for) is dependent upon its presuppositions to determine the inferential value of its major constructs.

6. To have established a premise is to have clarified the terminology upon which the premise is based.

Presupposition.

The presupposition, while absolute in intention, is relative in function; it is an essential component in the search for truth.

Presuppositions:
1. A presupposition serves the analytical process as the initial subject matter, providing an existent with potential meaning.
2. Characteristic of every presupposition is its intentionality.
3. A presupposition comes into being by means of reflective thought but functions on the cognitive level.

Principles.

Principles are ontological in nature because they are methodological conceptions.

Presuppositions:
1. The task of the *a priori* principle is to aid in the development of inferences. All *a priori* principles are analytical in nature.
2. The principles which underlie the science of epistemology also serve as the assumptions in the material of knowledge.
3. The primary concern of principles is with the relationships which exist between propositions.
4. Principles serve as the criteria of ideals; this implies that an ideal exists to bring other ideals into existence.
5. Inherent within every principle is the ethical postulate.
6. Every principle is explanatory; metaphysical principles serve as the ground of understanding.
7. Principles never develop into facts.
8. First Principles can be defined only in terms of purpose. To be a first principle implies that within its own being lies the

potentiality for self-justification.
9. Inherent within inductive principles is the power of self-correction.
10. Principles are logical when they are valid for all laws of reason.
11. Inherent in principles is the methodology to be used in explanation.
12. To synthesize principles is to be aware of the potentiality of the laws of logic.

Probability.

Probability is identification with perceived fact.

Presuppositions:
1. Evolving from the principles of verifiability is the concept of probability.
2. Probability and its perspective is subject to the process of interpretation in the validation of its structure.
3. Probability is a function of truth.

Problem.

When data challenges explanation, and the process of abstraction requires the conceptualization of value conditions, an epistemological problem has been posited.

Presuppositions:
1. To determine the structure of a problem does not necessarily imply the use of logic in the methodology employed.
2. To recognize a problem is to transcend it. Problems arise when one idea confronts another idea.

Procedure.

Both the inductive and deductive methods are approximate procedures.

Presupposition:

1. The quality of investigative procedure is dependent upon the potential inherent in the data.

Process.

Process is movement; movement evolves from cause, motivated by its inherent power. Process does not speak in terms of ends, only movement.

Presuppositions:

1. Every process is determined by causality.
2. Principles underlie every premise; it is the propositional principle which serves as the cause of process.
3. To experience is to learn; to learn is to understand by means of the conceptual process. It is this process which destroys the distinctiveness of the fact.
4. To possess knowledge of the implications of the creative process is to have enabled the self to validate conclusions.
5. The creative process functions only by means of living organisms; to make each of these organisms functional is to make them causative; to make them causative is to provide them with the opportunity to be creative.
6. The creative process is dependent upon the intellect for its direction.
7. The creative process is rational because it is dependent upon natural means for expression.
8. From essence evolves the source of the creative process; to function, it is dependent upon language and thought.
9. The creative process requires time.
10. All presuppositions are absolute in nature, scope and purpose; while they give birth to that which is relative, it is only on the sense of becoming that a process depends upon relativity for its momentum.

11. While creation expresses order, the determinant in the creative process is value.
12. In every process, the inferential function is present; it is this factor which gives to the process its ontological character.
13. The co-determinants of the intellectual process are will and intelligence.
14. One responsibility of the intellectual process is abstraction; the other is isolation.
15. Each stage in the investigative process is dependent upon the preceding stage for the completion and fulfillment of its intention.
16. If representation exists as an integral part of the knowing process, it is the process itself which must determine the truth of its significance.
17. The learning process works toward an idea.
18. The learning process moves on the assumption that alternatives exist in every theory.
19. An integral part of the learning process is the confrontation which must take place between facts.
20. To define meaning is the goal of the learning process.
21. Means and methods are integral parts of any metaphysical process.
22. All process, by its nature, implies the presence of a creative potential.
23. Depth in the reasoning process depends upon depth in experience.
24. Process is teleologically based.
25. The organization of the thought process is dependent upon the organization of principles affecting theories.

Properties.

An attribute of properties is determined by the conditions out of which values evolve.

Proposition.

To analyze a proposition is to discover the principles undergirding its structure, thereby determining its potentiality for identification with other propositions.

Presuppositions:

1. To analyze the structure of a proposition is to examine its scope to determine its inherent relationships.
2. Inherent within the proposition is the anticipatory perspective.
3. Inherent within a proposition are the assumptions which must be true if they are to serve in that capacity as conditions.
4. To actualize itself as being the proposition must reflect its image as a universal.
5. Propositions become meaningful when all of their constituent factors are seen one in relation to the other.
6. An empirical proposition is only probable.
7. An existential proposition is inherent in every concept.
8. Propositions open the potentiality of experience.
9. All factual propositions evolve from logical connectives.
10. The structure of propositions is dependent upon internal causal relationships to provide form and content.
11. To have determined the genesis of a proposition is to have determined cause.
12. The proposition inherent in the value judgment is determined (for the sake of its meaningfulness) by the metaphysical implications of its goal.
13. A proposition is related by and structurally based upon its implications.
14. Inherent in every proposition are the directives which evolve from intention.
15. In every proposition can be found the evidence for its

justification.
16. A proposition is always justified because of its presuppositions.
17. All metaphysically based propositions are hypothesized as law.
18. Inherent in every proposition is the law of contradiction.
19. To determine the limits of a proposition, the inductive method must be used.
20. Inherent within the proposition is the methodology necessary for the logical expression of its meaning.
21. The meaningfulness of a proposition is realized when the proposition itself is structured meaningfully.
22. Every metaphysical proposition depends upon a historical context to give it meaning.
23. Presupposed in every metaphysical proposition is a law, logical in nature, which reveals the truth of the proposition.
24. The metaphysical proposition is dependent upon empirical proof for its validation.
25. As existents, every proposition and object has a value character.
26. Propositions reveal purpose.
27. The qualification of a proposition is the generalization of its particulars.
28. The quality of a proposition is found in its meaning.
29. To determine the relationship between propositions is to determine the potential inherent in their causal conditions.
30. To determine and define relationships between propositions is to be concerned with the validation of those relationships.
31. To perceive the structure of a proposition is to be conscious of the causal concept underlying its intention.
32. Inherent within the proposition is a synthesis delineating a particular. The power to synthesize evolves from the power of integration.

33. To verify a proposition is to perceive an existent by means of the process of awareness.
34. The true proposition is the validated fact.
35. Fact recognized as principle evolves from the validated proposition.
36. In his search for truth, the learner is dependent upon the validation of propositions.
37. Every proposition possesses implicative values; the teleological premises of these values provoke the need for reflective thought.
38. Any proposition designates facts in relation to one another; to accomplish this, the proposition is dependent upon the methodology inherent in the process of verification.

Purpose.

Purpose is founded upon the principle of consistency.

Presuppositions:
1. Purpose functions only as belief functions.
2. Purpose evolves from the realization of cause.
3. Evolving from purpose is the law of conformity.
4. Purpose is the working assumption underlying explanation.
5. To function, purpose must relate to some facet in the material of knowledge.
6. It is purpose that controls the intent of a hypothesis.
7. Purpose, to validate its intention, cannot be divorced from its ethical ends.
8. Purpose is dependent upon sequence in intention.
9. Purpose is found as an integral part of natural law.
10. Purpose is realized in order.
11. Within the structure of a proposition lies purpose; in the validation of purpose lies the determinative quality of potentiality.
12. The realization of purpose is implemented by an analysis of

the potentiality of an idea.
13. That which is purposive is structured by the relevance factor present in the relationship between universals.
14. To validate purpose is to verify its meaningfulness.

Q

Qualities.

Qualities evolve from experiential relationships inherent in value conditions.

Presuppositions:

1. Qualities evolve from natural situations.
2. All qualities are rational.
3. All qualities are perceived by the understanding inherent in introspection.
4. Qualities are universals.

Quality.

Abstraction is presupposed in the structure of quality. While quality is characteristic of all that which has been created, quality is a relational tenet of two factors becoming integrated for a larger purpose.

Presuppositions:

1. Quality has, as its working hypothesis, the inherent structure in objectivity.
2. Quality *is,* because it is a quality.
3. Quality is the essence of substance.
4. To expand quality is to develop meaning.
5. To validate a quality, perception must verify the principles which determine relationships.
6. Evolving from the value condition is the construct of quality.

R

Reaction.

A reaction, to be perceptive, must call into being its power for subjectivity.

Presupposition:

1. Indicative of quality in any reaction is the depth of experience encountered in relationships.

Real.

What is real is dialectical.

Presuppositions:

1. Only the real can be experienced by the mind.
2. Only that which is real can expand an ideal.

Realism.

Realism, like idealism, relies heavily on the powers of the imagination for determining potentiality.

Presupposition:

1. Realism carries within its own stance the power for interpretation as well as for reproduction.

Reality.

Reality is found only in relation to an absolute.

Presuppositions:

1. Reality is actualized when recognized as a value concept.
2. The relationship between the experiential values of reality and the experiential values of appearance is one of synthesis.
3. Reality is a category without lines of demarcation.

4. Stratification is not a characteristic of reality; reality is being; this means reality is a totality.
5. Reality is the presupposition of any existent.
6. To determine the basis of reality, the learner must recognize that he is an integral part of the object of the search.
7. All reality is coherent and consistent.
8. The nature of reality is dependent upon the facts of consistency in the structure of its purpose.
9. The nature of reality is determined by the value condition and as ordered by the essence of its structure. The essence of reality is spiritual; it is determined by its function.
10. Reality, existence and essence are identical.
11. There is nothing beyond experience; reality is experiencing its existent.
12. It is the material of knowledge which determines, by means of its concepts, the ideal of reality.
13. Reality presupposes an internal unity within its own structure.
14. Reality is the unity of knowledge.
15. Only what is real can explain the meaning of reality.
16. All reality presupposes a metaphysical base; it is from this base that the evolutionary process postulates its potentiality.
17. Reality implies the unification of a process, the actualization of a method empirically structured.
18. Reality is determined by the ability of the mind to discern relationships between parts as inter-dependent factors.
19. The nature of reality is determined by means of the function of the cognitive act.
20. The object of perception is reality; reality is actualized only by means of perception.
21. The potential in reality is to presuppose the nature of reality.
22. Reality is the process of unifying and integrating facts.
23. Reality is teleologically based in purposive spontaneity.

24. Reality and substance are identical, based upon the same presuppositions which state that values and ideals are one and the same.
25. All methodology possesses a working metaphysical base; theory of reality evolves from methodology.
26. To actualize reality, the mind is concerned with the opportunity to objectify coherence and validity.
27. To test reality is to validate its historicity.
28. Reality is the subject of truth rather than its object.
29. Since value is experiential in function, it is the value judgment presupposed by the value condition which structures the nature of reality. Since reality is dependent upon the conditions of the value judgment for the validation of its meaning, the value judgment and the appraisal of the real are identical.

Reason.

Reason is the process of experience.

Presuppositions:

1. The goal of reason is to provide the mind with the intellectual setting for creativity.
2. It is the process of intellection which is the basic ingredient of reason; its function is the discovery of error.
3. The responsibility of reason includes both means and end. Because of this characteristic, it is able to synthesize all facets of its objects.
4. In determining the validity of a proposition, it is the process of actualizing the potentiality of probability which makes it possible for reason to structure its methodology.
5. Reason is the power of perception.
6. Reason is a process, not an acquisition.
7. To function, reason must be sensitive to the directives of the will.

Reason, cause.

Reasons are based on cause.

Reasoning.

In both inductive and deductive reasoning, there is movement from the principles of facts to meaning.

Reference.

Every frame of reference possesses a teleological responsibility; without it, there can be no ultimate frame of reference.

Presupposition:

1. To determine a point of reference is to put oneself at the omega point, thereby bridging two points by means of mind.

Referent.

Every referent is ontologically based, pointing to its own source of being.

Reflection.

To reflect is to experience the object of the mind's activity. Such activity implies the awareness of consequences under the direction of purpose.

Presuppositions:

1. Reflection actualizes an existent by determining its relevancy to an object already realized by the mind.
2. To learn, reflection is recognized as an integral part of the operative pattern of the mind.
3. Reflection is the brake of the mind of intellection refusing to accept every proposition proffered by intuition.
4. To reflect objectively is to conceptualize what is expressible.
5. The process of reflection includes an analysis of self-ability

in the handling of the working knowledge in hypotheses inherent in propositions.

Refutation.

The responsibility of refutation is to posit partially apprehended truths indicating their inadequacies for understanding the whole of fact.

Relation.

Universality is the pivotal condition underlying every causal relation.

Presupposition:
1. To determine a causal relation is to have determined the necessary criteria for the evolvement of all other relationships.

Relationship.

A relationship implies a transcendent unity actualizing reality through experience.

Presuppositions:
1. Relationships are expressed by creative laws.
2. To define a relationship, other relationships must be used in the construct.
3. The essence of any relationship is spiritual in conation.
4. Every relationship is instrumental in its nature, scope and purpose.
5. To determine a relationship is to have found meaning.
6. To structure a relationship is to perceive, via the process of synthesization, the cognitive values inherent in abstraction.

Relativism.

Relativism is merely a descriptive construct pointing to a lack of knowledgeable consequence.

Presupposition:
1. Even though the process of perception brings the learner higher on the scale of apprehension, there are degrees of relativism at all levels on the scale.

Relativity.

As objects imply the existence of subjects, relativity implies the existence of cause, the teleological principle of an absolute.

Presupposition:
1. To be conscious of relativity is to transcend it.

Reliability.

To determine reliability is to verify and validate by means of empirical evidence that which can be objectified; it is to be aware of its ontological nurture.

Requiredness.

What is required and why, and by whom for specific reasons, serve as the presuppositions underlying each value condition.

Research.

Research presupposes the need to collect and validate facts; these serve as assumptions in the methodology chosen; to make these facts transparent through the medium of interpretation is the next important step.

Presuppositions:
1. The chief function of research is to bring into being within the mind the capacity for creative insight.
2. While discovery and validation will always serve as the goals of research, the methodology underlying the process for the actualization of these goals possesses the need for assurance that the goal will serve, in turn, as the means for

the development of new ideas.
3. As education begins with a problem and learning is synonymous with experience, research is the means by which a question is tested for validity.
4. While in mind functions for the most part from a subjective base, it is the methodology of research which must maintain its objectivity.

Researcher.

The true researcher is the one who works toward the potential.

Resemblances.

Resemblances, like acquaintances, need substantiation. Appearances, like positations, require the use of basic assumptions; substantiated assumptions outline the premise underlying the relational status of resemblances.

Responsibility.

Responsibility in choice is its most important characteristic.

Revision.

Revision presupposes that use has been made of correct methodology in solving a given problem; the findings, based upon evaluating given bias provide the directives for re-evaluation or revision of the original hypothesis.

Rule.

A rule, separate in existence from a problem, does not give place to the inconsistent laws of nature or character.

S

Satisfaction.

Satisfaction is the resultant of the process of measuring the evidence of quality and finding it to be a value.

Schema.

Fulfillment is the aim of any expositional schema. Fulfillment contains within itself a value system thereby possessing a judgment factor for the measurement of completion.

Science.

To function, science as a methodology inherent in the material of knowledge becomes the construct of the mind which organizes its content according to the directives of the learning process. Only in this way is science able to function in a predictive sense.

Presuppositions:

1. Science, as the embodiment of the material of knowledge and its inherent methodology has, as its aim, comprehension; comprehension permits the mind to react aesthetically to the content of science.
2. The factors of cause and effect and their inherent relationship determine the aim of science.
3. To determine relationships among facts is the long range aim of science.
4. Science is a philosophy of being, a method for determining the reality of existence.
5. To function, science is dependent upon the fact; fact makes all science descriptive in nature.
6. To function, science is dependent upon the dialectic to provide structure.
7. Knowledge and its form is discovered by the creativity inherent in the process of discovery.
8. Inherent in the nature of empirical science is a responsibility for classification, the activity of which is purposive.
9. Science does not permit the recognition of entities; as such, it accepts the responsibility to analyze and determine the

validity of value condition, the determiner of what the knower can know.
10. The working hypothesis of science is faith.
11. The function of science is to reveal the relationship between things, and between things and the mind.
12. One function of science is predicated on its need to predict.
13. The function of science is to discover the transcendent purpose of the universe by means of the laws which govern its being.
14. To achieve the ideal of science is to reach the ideal inherent in every value condition.
15. The method of science is empirically based, primarily on the process of induction and secondarily on the process of deduction.
16. The dialectic is a basic methodology of science.
17. To actualize the potential of natural science is to experience its value conditions.
18. Science has as the prime objective of its nature the communication of content.
19. Science becomes operational when it compares one fact with another.
20. The perspective of science is dependent upon the value condition. Such a perspective is transitory in nature even though it is based on the techniques inherent in its methodology.
21. Science is the embodiment of its essence and as such functions only within the perspective of fact.
22. While science possesses its own methodology for the solution of its problems, its philosophy, with its own methodology, proffers the need to understand the objective of science.
23. To be conscious of the potentiality of science is to understand its processes.

24. The premise of science is one of condition: that which has been created evolved from a unified source or cause; order, arising from the creative process, implies coherence and unity.
25. Description as well as explanation serve as the dual object of science.
26. The responsibility of science is to determine only universal truths; only in this manner is it able to actualize its function.
27. Social science as the applicability factor in the value judgment functions only by means of the conditions which give it relevance.
28. The starting point of science is the working hypothesis projected as fact; basic to the fact is its underlying proposition.
29. Science, as a system of thought, projects its essence by means of the abstract proposition.
30. One of the prime values of science is to provide direction to thought and its processes.
31. To verify function and purpose in science is to determine the implicative values inherent in its laws.

Scientist.

The working premise of the scientist is to determine the nature of each law relevant to each fact and its dependencies; it is the natural law which serves as the connective between facts. In this way alone can he determine the creative element inherent in the rules of experimentation.

Presupposition:

1. The responsibility of the scientist is to recognize his need to actualize his bias and presuppositions before proceeding to analyze the rules of logic under which he must function.

Scope.

Scope implies a reality based on actuality however insufficient for actualization; the potential develops the adequacy needs of the object.

Search.

The search in analysis presupposes a need for clarity, in turn to be achieved through the choice of methodology. Its purpose is to free the researcher from bias and enable him to recognize truth.

Selection.

Selection implies an explanation by means of categorization.

Self.

To bring the self into a knowledgeable relationship to an organismically structured part is to identify parts with a whole.

Presuppositions:
1. The self is realized only in relation to what is experienced, and becomes a contributory unit in the process of human understanding.
2. Self-generating refers to the opportunity thus provided the learner for self-realization.
3. The self is both means and end.

Self-Realization.

Self-realization is the aim of experience; experience is realized through meaning.

Presupposition:
1. Self-realization is the resultant of the act of causation.

Semantics.

Differences in the use of words or of their combinations demand, on the part of the user, a sensitivity to meanings as implied in applicative connotations.

Sensate.

The principles underlying the process of apperception are the same which identify the sensate with the metaphysical.

Sensation.

All sensation is dependent upon the thought process for expression.

Sensations.

Sensations are reactions formulated by mind alone.

Presupposition:
1. Sensations, to be actualized, must be experienced to determine quality.

Senses.

The senses reflect all reaction via the mind; if the senses have subjected themselves to the whims of mere illusions, it is the mind which must do the correcting through the process of intellection.

Sensitivity.

Sensitivity is an attribute bearing judgmental value. As an attribute it assumes the character of a process of awareness which reveals to the inquiring mind the potentiality of the known.

Sequence.

Sequence and time are the means whereby causality reveals its nature.

Similarity.

Similarity suggests the need for likenesses to be characterized by a potential for application to a given object.

Simplification.

Simplification is the process of reducing quantity to its limits and developing quality to its fullest potential.

Skepticism.

Skepticism provides the braking power for the learner in his relationship with a new idea. It permits the "thinking time" necessary for reviewing the implicative values in reactions to what posits itself as truth.

Solution.

The solution of any problem is dependent upon the formulation of the problem.

Specialization.

Specialization begins with the beginning of creativity; it can assume its responsibility only when the meaning of the whole is understood.

Specificity.

To perceive is to suggest the presence of specificity.

Speculation.

Speculation requires the use of reflective thinking; it develops from observation.

Spontaneity.

Spontaneity is an expression emanating from the experience gained from explanation.

Presuppositions:

1. The process of intention as well as internalization makes it possible for spontaneity to evolve.
2. The spontaneity which brings intuition to fruition is imagination.

Statement.

A statement is an unvalidated proposition.

Presuppositions:

1. An analytical statement is a proposition which has related meaning and its object.
2. It is the statement which is the most definitive that suggests the use of the imagination.
3. The first test of the true statement is recognition; this premise is posited because of the analytical nature of a true statement.
4. A statement is true when it corresponds to another statement that has already been validated.
5. Until a statement has been verified, it is at best a hypothesis. Before a statement can be verified, its probability must be determined.

Stipulation.

Stipulation is based on understanding the meaning of a given object, the truth of which is made evident through its intuitive directive.

Structure.

Structure implied in any construct is based on the quality of internal relationships.

Presuppositions:

1. It is impossible to structure or to organize a system unless there is inherent within both the means which relate one fact to another.
2. To structure is to actualize potentiality.

Study.

Inherent within the perspective of study is its recognition of the commonalities in means and end.

Subject.

In empiricism, the subject is considered as fact; this implies that the empiricist has experienced the structure of the fact by means of relationships.

Presuppositions:
1. To determine meaning in or for either, the subject and object are mutually dependent upon one another; the one presupposes the existence of the other.
2. Subject and object are inter-dependent because they condition one another.
3. It is impossible to abstract either subject or object from their relationships.

Subjectivity.

Subjectivity is the setting in which every experience actuates itself.

Substance.

Substance retains its essence even though it may change.

Presuppositions:
1. Essence, therefore substance, is replete in that which is absolute.
2. Substance is to be found behind every change.
3. When substance changes, it functions as a correlative of parts.
4. The essence of substance implies its existence. All substance is preternatural in essence.

Substantives.

All substantives are particulars.

Presupposition:
1. Substantives must be used in deriving meaning from concepts.

Sufficiency.

To determine the principle of sufficiency is to depend upon the unifying traits inherent in a system.

Suppositions.

Suppositions do not require belief in their tenets.

Presupposition:

1. Within each supposition lies an alternative structured by the value condition alone.

Symbol.

The creativeness of a symbol lies in its ability to determine its own image.

Presuppositions:

1. As both means and end, the symbol reflects the end within its means or functional ability.
2. The purpose of any symbol is to suggest the potential in an existent; the symbol then, functions only by means of its anticipating perspective.
3. Symbols ascribe meaning to relationships.
4. Symbols serve to enforce reactions which, in turn, serve as the intrinsic motivation for intuition.

Symptom.

Each fact is an integral part of a whole and each whole is a universal; a system, based on universals is therefore open and compatible as one fact is open to and compatible with another fact.

Synopsis.

Synopsis is a responsibility of the scientific method.

Presupposition:

1. Synopsis fulfills the perspective of analysis.

Synthesis.

Synthesis is a correlation of what first appears as entities.

Presupposition:

1. The creative synthesis is a synthesis of qualities.

System.

An integrated system implies that its parts have retained a distinctive identity, but each part is dependent upon another for its functional aptitude.

Presuppositions:

1. The purpose of constructing a system is to determine points of validation whereby a problem is solved when ideas gained through insight are brought to birth.
2. In the structure of a system it is the underlying presuppositions which serve as the determinants in the process of validation.

Systematize.

To systematize is to enable the mind to develop principles which structure relationships which are organismic in nature; it is to rely upon the structure inherent within comparability.

T

Tautology.

A tautology requires another tautology for the realization of purpose.

Teaching.

To teach is to provide the setting in which ideas become connected.

Technique.

A technique is a method whereby means and potentiality are linked, and each step is meaningfully absorbed in the next step.

Presuppositions:

1. Technique, as an art, receives its motivation from the subject of its inquiry.
2. Technique is means of expression.

Teleology.

Inherent within each postulate is the perspective of teleology. This factor rules out the presence of a mechanical characteristic for any postulate.

Presuppositions:

1. Cause is dependent upon principles; principles explain the determination of direction in teleology.
2. Chance is not a factor in the responsibility of teleology.
3. Knowledge does not exist without its teleological characteristic; it is this facet of its being which determines the reality of knowledge.
4. Meaning determines the quality of the perspective of teleology; quality alone determines direction.
5. Basic to the function and responsibility of teleology is its recognition of mind and the evolving factor of intention.
6. As a way of thought, teleology, dependent upon its intrinsic organismic perspective, is an inherent attribute of the mind.

Tendency.

Any tendency is conditioned by inherent trends.

Test.

The purpose of testing is to determine meaning.

Presupposition:

1. Inherent within a test is an operative methodology by means of which the test is enabled to test itself.

Theory.

Characteristic of theory is the objective nature of its relativity.

Presuppositions:
1. With the actualization of a theory, there is the projection of evernew potentialities. To actualize a theory is to determine the validity of its purpose.
2. The aim of theory is the discovery of truth.
3. All theory evolves from concepts in relation to facts and their principles.
4. Every relationship is actualized only by means of conceptual thought. It is from the connectives which structure relationships that theories evolve.
5. A theory does not ignore the implicative values found in every fact; interpretative theory bases its methodology upon inferences evolving from fact.
6. Inherent in every theory are patterns of thought generated by generalizations.
7. While the inductive theory of method is a science of methodology, it serves only to clarify the material of knowledge.
8. To experience the potentiality of a theory is to have deductively determined the scientific value inherent in its consequences.
9. The purpose of theory is to predicate fact.
10. It is theory that recognizes flux in reality.
11. A theory is an attempt to extract from facts an explanation of relationships.
12. A law is valid only in relation to another law; it is from this premise that theory derives its responsibility.
13. A scientific theory, which is personal in nature, as a

working hypothesis defines relationships between observable phenomena.
14. The structure of theory is based on its perspective actualized by its potentiality.
15. To defend a theory is to work with the value judgment.
16. To project theory is to project a definition.
17. True theory never by-passes fact; it makes every attempt to clarify the fact.
18. The theory infers truth.
19. Inherent in theory is its own value.

Thing.

A thing is real when it has been actualized by the mind, and the mind has determined its potentiality.

Presuppositions:

1. Knowledge of a thing implies that the essence of the thing is more extensive than the mind's knowledge of it.
2. All things are composed of pluralities, but inseparable and related by principles of unification.
3. Things are known when the relationship between things are known.
4. Things reflect the ontological being of the mind operating by means of the process of intellection.

Think.

To think is the initial step in developing the ability to conceptualize. To think using the symbols of abstraction is to conceptualize.

Presuppositions:

1. To think is to search for the ideal contained in truth.
2. To think reflectively is to destroy prejudice and validate the meaningfulness of an existent.
3. To think is to become involved in the relationships realized

in thought.

Thinker.

The creative thinker concerns himself with the ideals inherent in abstract formulae.

Thinking.

Thinking and its perspective for meaningfulness is dependent upon an ability to determine implicative value; thus, it demands the use of transcendence.

Presuppositions:

1. Thinking is always conditioned by the learning situation basic to thought itself.
2. Thinking is conditioned by the relationships engendered by its perspective.
3. Thinking takes place only in relation to an object or a system back of which bespeaks universals.

Thought.

All thought functions in a framework of comparative analysis; one thinks about the process of thought because he is a thinking person. Thus, all thought is based on presuppositions.

Presuppositions:

1. To prepare a value setting is the function of abstract thought.
2. Thought is the actualization of the real; it is the realization of being.
3. Wholes imply a totality organismically structured; complete thought is dependent on such an organism.
4. Fact is basic in the development of thought when structured by the deductive method.
5. All thought is dialectical in principle.
6. All dialectical thought is thinking toward cause.

7. All thought is grounded in being.
8. Thought and the generation of ideas as concepts are identical because of their dependency upon intuition.
9. Thought is brought into focus by means of the language employed.
10. Thought is the language of the mind.
11. The laws of thought are synonymous with the laws of logic.
12. Thought is the means whereby the learner unifies his life to determine its relevancies.
13. Experience unifies and integrates objective and subjective thought; both thought patterns serve to assure that the symbolic nature of language, to be effective in the learning process, must act in the capacity of causal forces in the mind.
14. All thought is ontologically based on existential truth.
15. The quest of human thought is to make it possible for its subject matter to determine its relationships.
16. Reflective thought gives rise to value conditions underlying the formulative principles inherent in every problem.
17. Reflective thought is dependent upon the objective levels of analysis for incentive.
18. Reflective thought and its cognitive processes depends upon data to structure its premises.
19. Reflective thought uses data as reality factors in determining the relevancy of quality.
20. Reflective thought is the means by which the idea has been created.
21. The resultant of thought is a concept; it is the concept which must be verified in experience.
22. Scientific thought functions by means of its inherent concepts.
23. It is spontaneity of thought which characterizes the cutting edge of perception.

24. A system of thought imposes upon itself specific delimitations; these are in accordance with implied presuppositions concerning the nature of truth.
25. To construct a system of thought is to reduce concepts and place them in order of meaning.
26. To determine progress in thought is to reveal its nature by understanding its aim.

Time.

Time is identical with the "consciousness" factor of the individual.

Presuppositions:

1. It is the time factor in an act or event which permits the mind to relate two or more facts.
2. Time has, as one of its responsibilities, the constant delineation of factors separating object from subject.
3. Time exists because its structure presupposes the presence of potentiality.

Totalities.

Totalities come into being and function via the mind only when the material of knowledge has been fully comprehended.

Totality.

In every totality there is a determinant underlying the unity of universality even though it might imply a unity of differences.

Presuppositions:

1. Totality implies harmony between subject and object conditions.
2. Metaphysics is the working base of totality; it provides its perspective.

Tradition.

Tradition is dependent upon transition to determine its historicity.

Transcend.

To transcend is to have determined potentiality by uniting will and knowledge.

Presupposition:
1. To transcend is to have realized the potentiality of a perspective by structuring its futurity.

Transcendence.

To exist implies the presence of the potential of transcendence.

Presuppositions:
1. Not even the process of transcendence is free from presuppositions.
2. Transcendent thought is the means whereby a hypothesis determines the validity of a fact by transcending it but contradicting its essence.
3. Self-transcendence requires the human mind to experience the conditioning force of an object, the material of which reveals its structure and identity to the learner, the quality of projection realized through the process of awareness.
4. To function beyond the immediate is to transcend the subject of thought.
5. To transcend is itself the resultant of a value judgment.

Truth.

The essence of the material of knowledge is the embodiment of truth.

Presuppositions:
1. Truth is the realization of an abstraction.
2. To actualize truth is to realize the potentiality of understanding.
3. Truth is actualized in experience because of its relevancy

and meaningfulness in relation to another dimension of truth.
4. Truth implies appreciation.
5. To apprehend truth the mind requires the use of the analytic method.
6. Truth is absolute; herein lies its only value.
7. Truth unites the absolute and the relative.
8. Truth, as the material of knowledge, is implied in the nature of any whole.
9. Truth is value; as such, it brings into being self-realization and fulfillment.
10. The assumptions of truth are unconditional.
11. To attain truth is to arrive at a point in the mind set where contradiction is no longer a factor in the process of intellection.
12. To determine the significance of being is to determine the meaningfulness of truth.
13. Truth is the realization of being in the absolute sense.
14. The cause of truth is not dependent for its existence upon its recognition.
15. Truth is dependent upon the cause in each condition to determine its relevancy and meaning.
16. Truth is realizable through the analytical power of the concept.
17. To conceptualize truth is to determine its function.
18. Truth has its conditions making its existence possible.
19. The content of truth cannot be changed by the human mind.
20. To define truth is to determine its conditions.
21. Truth possesses a definitive nature.
22. One statement, combining the Analytic and the synthetic, is the only means whereby truth can be described.
23. Truth is determined by the degree of awareness of the implicative values in life.

24. Empirical truth is probable truth.
25. The essence of truth is realized only by means of its being.
26. Truth equates fact and belief.
27. The function of truth is to explain the material of its knowledge.
28. Truth, while independent of human thought for its existence, relies on human thought for its realization.
29. Truth transcends human will.
30. Truth, when deduced from a hypothesis, in reality has been deduced from fact.
31. Truth is the chief quality of judgment.
32. Truth, when analyzed by means of its tautological structure, justifies its nature when essence is identified with existence.
33. Since truth is always factual in structure and content, its premises are logical in nature.
34. The material of truth is the material of knowledge; as such, it generates experience and its meaning.
35. The material of truth is the substance of its being.
36. Truth is the realization of meaning.
37. Metaphysical truth is pure thought postulated abstractly.
38. Inherent within truth is its basic need for constant movement and progression.
39. Inherent within the nature of truth are those criteria which quite literally force it to be self-corrective and continuously validate its working presuppositions.
40. The nature of truth is dependent for its actualization by the mind upon the ability of the mind to conceptualize the potentiality of research as an art.
41. The nature of truth is identical with its synthetic quality.
42. Within the scope of method lies the need to synthesize all tenets arising from the dialectic of logic; this implies that all truth is tautological in nature.
43. Truth has as its object the strengthening of the human mind.

44. Truth is not subject to opinion nor based upon its assumptions.
45. Perceptive truth is truth apprehended as a concept.
46. The potential of truth is dependent upon human thought.
47. Truth is predicated on its cause.
48. The presupposition of truth is its absoluteness.
49. Faith is one presupposition of truth.
50. The prime responsibility of truth is to reveal its purpose.
51. Truth is never replaced by probability.
52. As a proposition, truth refuses to allow itself to be placed in a setting conducive to closure; since it is dependent upon the perspective of transcendence, truth, to remain truth, must be open on all sides.
53. The quest for truth requires the use of an assumption, namely, experience and meaning are synonymous as concepts in the learning process.
54. Truth is reality; what is real is the embodiment of truth.
55. Truth determines the nature of what is real.
56. In the process of learning, the major presupposition is that truth in each of its dimensions reveals reality.
57. Truth is realized when its meaning is absorbed by the mind.
58. Truth is teleological in nature, scope and purpose; its reason for existence is to bring into being other dimensions of truth.
59. Truth is meaningless without a referent.
60. It is the relevancy of truth and its many degrees of apprehension which structure the ideal and the means for its realization.
61. Rules of procedure are integral factors in the conceptualization of truth.
62. Truth cannot be typed nor can its content be classified; science concerns itself with truth as a totality.
63. The scope of truth is infinite.

64. Truth demands a setting for its comprehension; a system of thought provides this setting.
65. The significance and implication of truth is dependent upon the mind for its realization.
66. The standard of truth is absolute.
67. A statement of truth is dependent upon an empirical concept to give it meaning and relevancy.
68. To structure truth is to have determined its purpose.
69. The substance of truth is actualized by its dependent relationships.
70. Truth is the embodiment of all verified antecedent suppositions.
71. Truth possesses a historicity which transcends time.
72. To intuit truth is to become aware of its subjective qualities.
73. Truth, as the only universal, is abstracted in the revelatory power of the material of knowledge.
74. Truth speaks of itself; it determines its own validity. Truth, to be meaningful, must validate itself in reference to the absolute and its promises.
75. Degrees of the evolvement of value are present in every degree in the apprehension of truth.
76. Every value of truth is utilitarian in nature.
77. Truth is the only means for the verification of value in truth.
78. The verification of truth is actualized at the moment faith is actualized.
79. There is no such thing as a half-truth; truth is always complete and whole.

U

Ultimate.

The basic premise on which the ultimate is reached is the logical nature of its particulars.

Understanding.

Understanding is the judge of experience.

Presuppositions:
1. Understanding, to be actualized, must be realized in experience.
2. The learner understands as he validates the material of knowledge.
3. The material of knowledge provides the means for understanding.
4. It is understanding and its methodology which dissects the body of fact.

Unification.

In unification, no units are subordinate.

Uniformity.

Uniformity requires the explanation inherent in relational principles to declare its structure valid.

Unify.

To unify is to become aware of the implicative values of the absolute.

Presuppositions:
1. Unity evolves from the teleological principles at work in cause.
2. Within every descriptive factor characterizing a unity lies an analogous tenet characterizing a distinctive quality.
3. The nature of unity suggests there is no difference between past, present and future events.
4. Organic unity implies that use has been made of the regulative factors inherent in the process of becoming.

Universality.

Universality is a categorical imperative in the metaphysics of cause.

Presuppositions:

1. Universality is the working base from which a philosophy of education operates.
2. Universality is the working premise out of which metaphysics evolves as a science.

Universals.

Universals bespeak a need to be realized; their actualization is achieved through knowledge sensed in its contextual form.

Presuppositions:

1. Universals are confirmed by particulars.
2. The universal is the totality of wholes.
3. Inherent within the nature, scope and purpose of each universal is the extensional as well as the intensional dimension.

Universe.

The universe is the manifestation of the process of creation.

Presuppositions:

1. The chief attribute of the universe is the regularity of its unchangeableness.
2. The functional premise underlying the teleological perspective of the universe is this: relativity operates only under the metaphysical directives of the absolute.
3. It is the integrative qualities of the universe which makes unity on any level possible.
4. The universe exists to support the learner in personalizing the process of learning.
5. Because of its purposive nature, the universe is self-

experiencing through the meaning it transmits to the observer.
6. The universe remains an existential whole.

University.

The university is a projection, the resultant of a relationship between the inquiring mind and its search for, and application of, knowledge.

Unreality.

Unreality posits a need to be recognized as possessing reality to prove the unreal proceeds from this premise.

V

Validity.

Within the nature, scope and purpose of logic is a methodology generated by its own needs; it is this methodology which structures meaning in validity.

Presupposition:

1. In considering the problem of validity, the value condition must be taken into account.

Value.

To bring value into being is to realize meaning by means of its power for instrumentation; this means that value and reality are identical.

Presuppositions:

1. When a value judgment has been made, value has been experienced, therefore, actualized.
2. A value which has been definitively analyzed is one which

has been imperatively described.
3. As means and ends are identical in any value condition, the same may be said to be true with respect to value and being.
4. Value is being and a way of becoming.
5. There is no dualism between value and cognition.
6. Value is conditioned by its meaning; the quality of the conditioning process is dependent upon the nature of the subject-matter; here is movement toward clarification for the purpose of rendering a judgment.
7. The construct of value implies a contextual dependency; its meaning is always intelligible as a concept.
8. To demonstrate value is for the self to accept its conditions.
9. The situation as a source of confrontation serves as the incentive for the evolvement of value and the recognition of its quality systems. Value evolves from ideas inherent in the universal.
10. To bridge value and fact is to determine the nature of cause in each construct.
11. The suggestion of value and its evolvement implies a moral commitment.
12. A value requires constant evaluation of its interpretative function.
13. Logic provides the structure in determining the construct of value and its judgmental responsibilities, this implies the need to determine relevancy.
14. What is valued becomes the meaning of value.
15. The nature of the value condition does not change with the change often taking place in the value judgment.
16. A value is behavioral in its perspective.
17. To increase value is to increase the conditions inherent in its potentiality.
18. Value lies in its productivity.
19. The most important quality of value is consciousness.

20. Inherent within the structure of value are two components, prediction and unification.
21. The teleological base of every value is the means-end relationship.
22. To value is to react to a proposition proffered by the mind, thereby becoming identical with the proposition; it is finding meaning by experiencing meaning. In this way experience is always positive.
23. Uniqueness suggests the evolvement of a value.
24. The validity of value is determined by a dependency upon the material of knowledge and the temporal nexus.
25. A value evolves only because it has been verified.
26. To will is to value.
27. Values are determined as measures of control in experience.
28. As values evolve, they emerge as absolutes but subject to change, at times becoming relative.
29. Values make it possible for other values to develop.
30. Values make it possible for more values to evolve.
31. Values are dependent upon facts for the purpose of validation.
32. The functional potential of any value lies only within its own social milieu.
33. All values are objective in intent.
34. To determine meaning in values is to judge the depth of experience.
35. Values are ideals of rationality.
36. Values have the responsibility to develop other values.
37. By reason of its teleological nature, all values are transcendental in purpose.
38. Values contain verifiable truths.

Valuing.

To value is to identify the meaningfulness of an object of thought with the validated need of the self; in this way it serves as an ideal.

Presupposition:

1. In the learning process, the need to value is self-evident; valuing, as a process, is dependent on the working relationship between means and end to determine its conditions for judgment.

Variables.

Inherent within every variable is the value condition.

Verification.

Verification, which is a criterion of truth, defines a procedure whereby the object is reduced to its fundamental nature and meaning.

Presupposition:

1. To verify is to meet all of the demands inherent in the construct of coherence.

Virtue.

What becomes the "known" factor in the learning process, realizes itself in the concept of virtue.

W

Whole.

The whole weaves the strands of meaning into a unification of parts.

Presuppositions:

1. It is the mind which determines the construct of the whole.
2. Metaphysical epistemology is the one means by which the whole is realized.
3. For the whole to reveal the structure of its parts, as well as the design of its set, the relevancy of the relationship

between parts must be determined.

Will.

The will is a determinative; as a determinative it is a directive.

Presupposition:
1. Will is the pivotal presupposition of both existence and truth.

Wisdom.

Wisdom implies the existence of an awareness of the implicative relationship between cause and effect, and of the resultant value discoveries inherent within the instrumentation of both cause and effect.

Word.

A word, descriptive in its symbolism, possesses the power to create new perspectives through the use of ideas.

Presuppositions:
1. A word is meaningful when its substance has been validated and its form declared superior.
2. The power inherent in a word lies in its ability to motivate the learner.
3. The purpose of the word is to sensitize the mind in preparation for conceptualization.
4. Meaning is achieved through concepts designed by words; this process is known as reasoning.
5. It is the associate potentiality of a word which determines its perspective.
6. Words translate meaning extracted from the relationship between observation and perception.
7. To use a word properly (within the specificity of its use) is to have realized the implicative values inherent in its origin.
8. The most characteristic aspect of words are the integral fact

or which delineate relationships.
9. While words may connote different values, each word has its particular use.

Work.

To work is to do so simulatively, bringing to each step the progress of the past and a vision of the whole.

World.

The World is a created, unified order, harmonious in system, with laws and essence structured dependently and which describes its evolving condition.

Writing.

Writing is the revelatory response of the mind in meeting the demand for expression.

Resources

If you enjoyed this book, may I ask a small favor? Please go back to Amazon and leave an honest review of *A Dictionary of Philosophical Concepts*. Reviews help us spread the word of Dr. Russell A. Peterson to the world more effectively, and sustain our efforts. We appreciate your continued support.

Thank you,
Barry J. Peterson